Daily Inspirations to Achieve Your Real Estate Investment Goals

Begin Each Morning Focused on Your Real Estate Investment and Management Goals

Linda Liberatore

© 2016 Linda Liberatore
All rights reserved.

ISBN-13: 9780692709870
ISBN-10: 0692709878
Library of Congress Control Number: 2016907852
Linda Liberatore, Schaumburg, IL

Daily Inspirations to Achieve Your Real Estate Investment Goals

I would personally like to recognize and express my gratitude to Erica Myles. Without Erica's countless hours and contributions to these articles, this book would not have been possible. Erica's creative voice and perfect style added real value to the passages. I could not have achieved this book without your help, Erica, and I thank you for your contribution to make it happen.

I am blessed to have the support of my husband, Tim; my daughters, Marissa, Jenna, and Karli; and my mother. Without their love, encouragement, and inspiration, I could not continue. Thank you to my parents for showing me how to cherish the love of family. I miss you, Dad, every day, but you have left me with so many blessed memories. I have had so many mentors on this journey who have been so incredibly kind and generous with their time and stories in the real estate world. Without your help, I would not be here today. To my clients, I cannot thank you enough for your trust in Secure Pay One each and every day.

Introduction

I wrote this book to share the positive energy, passion, and information it takes each day as you dive deeper into the real estate investment world. I have made a commitment to engage daily with the investors and sources who have contributed to this book. After starting my own daily morning commitment, I realized something. By sharing this idea, I might be able to help someone on his or her real estate journey. Those of you who know me personally know that my days are long, but I will never settle for less than 120 percent effort. I have listened and learned from countless real estate investors association (REIA) groups, lenders, agents, and professional speakers, in addition to my daily work. I have personally lived with the challenges of rental property and witnessed the continued success of investors. I know the grit and determination it takes to persevere in the real estate investment world.

Real estate investment still leads our great nation as the largest category of entrepreneurship. Tax laws, regulatory changes, and economic cycles are just a few of the challenges in the real estate investment world. Each day comes with a struggle and a success. My work performing professional services assists real estate investors looking to reach their next goals. Secure Pay One works with individuals from all walks of life and all parts of the country who are thankful they are not alone in their mission to provide housing and build their legacies.

Make it so easy you can't say no.

—Leo Babauta

Day 1: Why Here? Why Now?

As you start your investor journey, become aware of the people investing who are successful. Ask questions. Learn and build new habits. It is essential that you examine your daily habits and mark your progress with small changes. Start with a tiny habit and perform it every day. Consider allocating a specific time each day to finding and tracking a property in a specific area.
Build on your new habit and increase it. Do this until it is comfortable. You are building momentum. Don't expect perfection as you start. Top performers learn that if they fall off the daily pattern, they can jump back on quickly. Build your consistency and your patience. Focus on finding habits that are common to the majority of your mentors. New habits should become stress free. Measure the impact on your health, your energy, and your happiness. Learn how to combine your efforts, automate your tracking, and add visual charts. Stack your habits and double down on success.

Our self-esteem comes from our work ethic, not our results.

Day 2: What Is a *Resident*?

Many nightmare situations arise from a landlord not spelling out the time limit on when a "guest" becomes a resident. Standard leases usually specify two weeks. When residents allow family and friends to move in, consequences can include an increase in utility bills, illegal activity such as drug dealing, and unnecessary stress on neighboring tenants. Due to the rise in popularity of Airbnb, some tenants even tap into their entrepreneurial spirit and allow complete strangers to occupy their units. Make sure your lease includes a Use of Premises clause, which should require your written permission for additional occupants. This clause keeps existing tenants from moving in unapproved "family" (yeah, right) and keeps unemployed boyfriends or girlfriends from becoming rogue tenants.

If you want to slip into a round hole, you must make a ball of yourself.

Day 3: If a Family of Four Becomes a Family of Eight

Some landlords misinterpret, to their own disadvantage, the housing laws created to prevent discrimination based on familial status. It is your right as a landlord, however, to restrict the number of residents based on how many people were in the initial group of applicants. This means that if a family of four moves in, the lease should restrict usage specifically to those four people. The Use of Premises clause in a standard lease limits visits to less than fourteen days. To guard against resourceful tenants looking for a loophole, it goes on to clearly state only one visit per six-month period. This comprehensive clause also restricts the tenant from "carrying on any business, profession, or trade of any kind, or for any purpose other than private dwelling."

Change your mind each day.

Day 4: Who Is That Unfamiliar Face?

Wise landlords perform background and credit checks on rental applicants to get to know the type of people they are allowing to access their property and to share living space with other tenants. When approved tenants allow additional occupants unknown to the landlord to move into their units, they bypass your screening process. Some tenants avoid informing the landlord because they fear a rent increase. Other tenants, however, are aware of something in the person's background that would cause the landlord to refuse to rent to that person. Would you want a person like that living in your building? Landlords and property managers must constantly be on the lookout for tenants who stretch the boundaries of their leases by allowing unauthorized—and often unwanted—guests to overstay their welcome.

> Nothing in life is to be feared; it is only to be understood.

Day 5: Who Does Renter's Insurance Really Protect?

Consider the following scenarios: If, God forbid, you suffer a loss due to a fire or a flood, your owner's insurance probably won't cover tenants' personal property or the expenses they incur while the property is being repaired. If the tenant is burdened with out-of-pocket expenses, such as the cost of replacing lost or damaged items, collecting your rent on time becomes a hopeful fantasy. The frustration of expecting the landlord to replace uninsured items sometimes puts a strain on the landlord-tenant relationship. If your uninsured tenant causes damage affecting another tenant or a neighbor, the affected party might attempt to go after the landlord, who they believe has deeper pockets. You'll have enough to worry about in arranging for the repairs to your property without these additional concerns. Therefore, who does renter's insurance ultimately protect? *You*—the landlord.

You can't stop time.

Day 6: Be a Hero—Advocate for Renter's Insurance

Don't take for granted that everyone understands the ins and outs of renter's insurance. Put on your salesperson hat and lay out the advantages. Renter's insurance gives you piece of mind that funds will always be available in case of emergency. Setting aside a few dollars in savings for a rainy day is not enough. We all have good intentions, but tenants are only human. It's tough to resist the temptation to "borrow" those funds for another use.

Policies are very inexpensive and easy to obtain. For less than $200 a year, or $10 to $20 per month, a typical policy covers around $15,000 in property damage and $100,000 in liability. Finally, depending on the renter's auto insurance policy, the renter might be entitled to deeply discounted, or even *free*, renter's insurance. Most tenants probably don't even know it. Won't they be glad you told them?

People have the gift of choice.

Day 7: Allocating Payments to Protect Your Interests

When a tenant makes all payments according to the lease agreement, deciding how funds are designated is an easy task. But honestly, how often does that happen? We should be so lucky, my friend. Make sure your allocation-of-funds procedure is clearly spelled out in your lease, including the process for when payments are *not* received according to terms.

Define the priority of funds received. Incoming payments should first be applied to late fees, then to repairs for damages caused by the tenant, then to any outstanding utility bills relating to the tenant, and finally to any outstanding rent. By saving unpaid rent for last, you safeguard the tougher-to-collect money first. Suing a tenant is unpleasant. But if you must, it's a lot easier to convince a judge to award you with unpaid rent than unpaid late fees or unpaid utilities.

> Success is a few simple disciplines, practiced every day, while failure is simply a few errors in judgment repeated every day.
>
> —Jim Rohn

Day 8: Let's Go, Team!

To be a mediocre owner, all you need to do is buy some property, rent it out to the first person who applies, and keep your fingers crossed. This is done while standing alone, inside your bubble. Being a successful landlord, however, is a team sport. Surround yourself with knowledgeable partners. Vital members of your team include your mortgage broker, real estate agent, real estate attorney, property manager, contractor, and accountant. And remember: having a game plan is important, but a team is only as good as its captain. Communicate your goals and vision with your team, and victory will be in the bag. Managing your property can be done on your own, but you're less likely to be happy with the results. Don't go at it alone!

People generally see what they look for and hear what they listen for.

Day 9: The Benefits of a Partner

The real estate business is littered with scams, and it takes the skills of a tightrope walker to avoid them. Going in with a partner can be of benefit to you to reduce your risks. Having a partner splits the risk (and the profits), making real estate investing a more attractive business. When getting started, you may lack financial resources as you start up your business. Having a partner can reduce your spending and thus improve your resources. Doubling the analysis may help in navigating the minefield of poor deals. Your partner's eye may pick up something you missed. Every partner has strengths and weaknesses. If your partner has strengths that can cover your weaknesses, then you will make a winning combination. Real estate is a tough field and requires a lot of running around. A partner goes a long way in helping divide these tasks. In addition, both of you bring your own set of contacts to the table, creating an expanded circle of networking. Accountability partners help in ensuring that personal milestones or problems do not encroach on the business and result in losses.

The only time you should ever look back is to see how far you've come.

Day 10: What Does Each Team Member Bring to Your Landlord Game Plan?

Each member of your team makes a unique and crucial contribution. Your mortgage banker or broker should offer the lowest possible interest rate and fastest closings. Your real estate agent should have specific experience understanding the needs of an investor and bring the best deals. Your real estate attorney should be experienced with the laws of rentals and how to handle an eviction. The property manager should know how to field service calls from tenants and keep them accountable for timely rent payments. The accountant should help you understand how to get all qualified deductions, as well as make sure your rental business is structured for maximum tax benefits. Finally, some landlords choose to have more than one trusted contractor on their contact list. Competition for your projects can foster greater accountability for completing projects on schedule and on budget.

Rise and grind.

Day 11: Property-Management Software

What good is it to buy top-of-the-line, state-of-the-art software if it takes too much time and effort to learn how to use it? Are you a quick study, or do you prefer a package that comes with technical support? Many advanced products have a lot of bells and whistles that you probably won't ever use. Don't opt for the added expense of something you don't even need. Consider which features are most important to you. Are there any hidden costs when you need assistance? Does the package offer a trial version or an option to "try before you buy"? No matter which product you choose, you should, of course, make sure that it provides the basics. But don't forget that it should leave room for add-ons that can allow your business to grow into a multimillion-dollar operation.

I will not be outworked.

Day 12: Empower Your Tenants to Make Your Building a Crime-Free Zone

The vast majority of renters want to live in safe, crime-free properties. However, renters often feel disconnected from the process. Many view crime prevention as the landlord's job. Some forgo neighborhood-watch meetings because they feel they're geared toward owners. If they fear they're in it alone, residents might fail to report crime. Help your law-abiding tenants feel empowered to take ownership of their living environment. Consider implementing crime-reduction programs specially designed for multiple-family buildings. Establishing relationships between police, owners, property managers, and residents in advance is the best way to squash problems before they start. Maintaining a good standard of living from the beginning helps to prevent those with criminal intent from ever getting a foothold.

Let your pain push you.

Day 13: Don't Get Stuck on Landlord Island

If you're new to investing and trying to decide on your first step, avoid drifting over to "Landlord Island." That's the place where many landlords end up when they become too isolated. The benefits of networking to a real estate investor are too numerous to count. Seek out your local real estate investors association (REIA). REIAs can be found in almost all local real estate markets. They bring together builders, owners, investors, bankers, lawyers, contractors, and other interested parties to discuss tried-and-true investing strategies and other opportunities. REIAs offer a great chance to network and form mutually beneficial, professional connections. A REIA often proves to be a more reliable way to connect with industry experts than cold-calling from a phone book or using a web search. The potential of attracting new business and referrals from a sizable group can attract professionals who work harder to maintain a trustworthy reputation.

The battlefield is in your mind.

Day 14: Analysis Paralysis

You see them at real estate workshops and events. They come prepared with fancy portfolios and shiny, high-grade pens. Their expressions are serious and intense as they hang on the speaker's every word. They furiously scribble notes on every important point in the discussion. The high-tech ones use their smartphones or tablets to snap pictures of every PowerPoint slide. They're so thorough that they even note the questions asked by members of the audience. We call them the Note Takers. They appear to be individuals on serious business. The only problem is that if you talk to them a year later, you'll find out that they haven't made a single move. Research and preparation are extremely important, but don't get so bogged down in the planning stage that you never take action to advance your real estate career.

God gave you two ears and one mouth, so you can listen twice as much as you're heard.

Day 15: The State of Supply and Demand

In a way, the real estate market is the truest marker of the state of the economy. Information is everywhere, the ABC's of economics can tell you, and supply always levels off to meet demand. Prices are directly driven by demand. In the United States, as a rule, the demand is at its peak during summer. It's important not to miss this window. But even the savviest of property investors can miss the boat because the process from fulfilling legal demands to finding a tenant can consume more time than expected. Consider Washington, DC, where millennials with high salaries are calling the shots and demanding homes in the city. In 2015, the city saw the highest sales of houses since the 2008 recession. To become a landlord in Washington, DC, you must purchase a basic business license, ensure proper inspection, and clear a variety of zoning and safety tests before marketing a property to tenants. So, start preparing for the peak season now, or it will be too late.

Do what is easy, and you'll become a victim.

Day 16: Crowdfunding: the Next Big Wave

Crowdfunding has been gaining buzz in real estate investing in recent years. The *Oxford Dictionary* defines it as "the practice of funding a project or venture by raising many small amounts of money from a large number of people, typically via the Internet." Crowdfunding can be a simple way to explore investing in your pajamas. It allows you to avoid driving all over town to view properties for sale. You can also bypass those open houses with disposable booties. You can browse different types of investments—homes, apartments, retail stores, office buildings—from the convenience of your laptop or smartphone. Remember: although it allows for more arm's-length investing for those who want to be less hands on, crowdfunding is still a form of investing. Always do your research. Grab your bunny slippers, fire up the coffeemaker, and check out what's available with the click of a button.

Your fight is your fuel.

Day 17: Forgive Yourself and Then Learn from Your Mistakes

Being a landlord takes a lot of guts. Many people dream about it, but only the bravest take action. Owning property involves many decisions. You can't expect to always make the right ones. When you make a mistake, first applaud yourself for having the courage to try. Then look for ways to choose a better solution if faced with the situation again. Research the issue online. Find books on the subject. Talk to other owners or local real estate professionals. If you find someone you can trust, be candid and explain the situation. Try not to be embarrassed or defensive when someone offers advice. You might be surprised to find out how many others have made the same mistake before you. The most experienced, successful landlord is often the one who made the most mistakes before finding the right path.

Absorb failure and move forward.

Day 18: Being a Landlord Is Not a Popularity Contest—It's a Business

    A landlord is first and foremost a human being. Some of us have a natural tendency to want to socialize with other likeable people. It's fine to have friendly interactions with residents of your properties. Just be careful not to blur the lines. For example, it can backfire if you go out for drinks with a tenant on Saturday night and then show up to collect the rent on Monday morning. Barring the occasional wild office party, we generally avoid letting our hair down in a job setting where we're observed by bosses, subordinates, and coworkers. Landlord-tenant relationships should follow the same rules of decorum. So go ahead and attend that wedding or funeral if the tenant thinks highly enough of you to invite you. Just don't lose sight of the fact that the foundation of your relationship is a business one.

Life shrinks or expands in proportion to one's courage.

Day 19: Your Phone System Can Reduce Your Stress and Make You Look like a Pro

Your direct-mail campaign has been wildly successful. Now the calls are streaming in, and you're losing your voice. Don't panic. Remember that success is a phone that rings off the hook, but make sure you're set up to handle that volume. Services such as Grasshopper let you create unique recorded messages for each of your properties or business ventures. Callers can navigate a supersimple phone menu to hear details about a property of interest.

One particularly helpful feature converts voice mails to e-mails or faxes for a quick reference to who is trying to reach you. With monthly plans starting as low as twelve dollars, you can even set up a toll-free number to increase the chances that potential customers will respond to your highly professional marketing efforts. Grab yourself some hot tea with lemon to soothe your throat and then use technology to make your job easier.

Take intention to action.

Day 20: Learn to Spot a Bad Situation Early

Good ol' Ben Franklin said it best: "A stitch in time saves nine." Recognizing and addressing a potential issue before it gets worse is your best bet for damage control. Chronic late payments are a sure sign that a tenant cannot afford your unit, or that the tenant mismanages income. In either case, don't ignore this red flag and wait for things to get better. Tenants make promises that they might even want to believe themselves. They might base promises to pay on expected legal settlements, work bonuses, or inheritances. Short of winning the lottery, what's the likelihood that a tenant will suddenly have the ability to pay off his or her mounting debt? Don't get taken in by a string of empty promises. Make efforts to get rid of nonpaying tenants before even more of your lost rent is at stake.

Today is your day. Your mountain is waiting, so get on your way.

Day 21: Having a Website Builds Credibility

Creating websites is so easy and inexpensive, and it seems as if everyone has one these days. There's a reason for that. Websites lend credibility. In some areas, businesses or investors without websites are viewed with raised eyebrows.

Some companies even allow people to set up basic websites for free in exchange for allowing them to include their names at the bottom of the pages. There's no need to hire someone to create a website for you. Sites such as Weebly.com and GoDaddy.com even offer templates and "wizards" that guide you through the process, step by step. Whether you're someone who has been in the business for decades or you have just finished your first book on getting started as an investor, think about setting up your site right away. There's nothing to lose except for the few hours it takes to set it up, but you never know what you might gain.

Our choices will be hard.

Day 22: "Oh, It's You...Again."

Landlords have certain expectations of the people who rent from us. These expectations include timely rent payments, prompt notifications of repair issues, and responsiveness to our attempts to contact them. It's only fair that tenants are entitled to expectations of us. The right to privacy and quiet enjoyment of their living space rank high on the list of tenants' expectations. Always try to adhere to a two-day advance notice for access. Not only is it an industry standard, it's also a good way for a landlord to show respect for the tenant's right to feel comfortable. The common landlord practice of "just dropping in" to watch for potential problems is considered obnoxious or even harassment by the average tenant with good intentions. Proper notice demonstrates that you, as the landlord, are a guest (although a necessary one) and encourages a healthy sense of "ownership" for the tenant.

Greatness is a lot of small things done well.

Day 23: My Rented Home Is Still My Castle

A landlord must balance the need to maintain the physical structure of the rental unit with the awareness of the tenant's emotional connection to "home." Try to anticipate how you can address situations before you have an urgent need to access the unit. If you consider how many issues really fall under the category of an "emergency," you might find that many could have been prevented with a little forethought. The key is proper planning and organization. Whenever possible, perform multiple tasks at one time to limit the number of visits to the tenant's home. Schedule routine checks of all systems (plumbing, electrical, heating/ventilation, etc.) and major appliances. This saves the tenant the embarrassment of snatching pantyhose down from the shower rod at the last minute when something breaks down. It also saves time, gas, and effort for *you*.

Wake up and go to bed with a thankful heart.

Day 24: Common Courtesy Breeds Goodwill

Two situations where a landlord is *not* required to give notice for accessing a unit include emergencies and building repairs that cause an unexpected need to enter the unit. Even when last-minute entry cannot be avoided, you can make the situation less intrusive. When the tenant is not at home, call, text, or e-mail the patron at the moment you're preparing to enter. Follow up with the tenant as you're leaving; let the tenant know that the unit is locked and secured. Most local laws allow you two days after entry to report, but that's two full days when the tenant might ask you about it first. If the tenant asks before you have a chance to disclose, the tenant is more likely to question whether you ever planned to inform him or her. Going above and beyond the minimum requirement is free and breeds goodwill.

I want it—I work for it.

Day 25: Why Is the Plumber Wearing My...

Even if you work hard to build trust with your tenant, an outside party could come in and strike a serious blow to your relationship. Some tenants fear stolen property in cases where the landlord gives access to a third-party contractor and leaves that person in the unit unattended—and for good reason. There have been documented cases of unsupervised tradespeople committing theft, making long-distance phone calls, and engaging in other abuses while performing work in a tenant's absence. First, strongly encourage the tenant to have a friend or family member present during repairs. If that's not possible, assure the tenant that you or your trusted property manager will remain in the unit until work is completed by a third party. Knowing that you care helps to make tenants more cooperative.

The best way to shape the future is to influence it.

Day 26: A Nosy Landlord "Making Repairs"

"Oh no! There was a break-in!" she says, after walking into her home following a late night at work. She knows her living space, and a few things are not as she left them.

"Nahhh!" says her neighbor across the hall, fumbling with his keys. "It was just the landlord. He does that all the time."

Tenants commonly suspect that landlords and repair people come and go at will when tenants are away from home. In many cases, unfortunately, it's a reality.

Some tenants living under these conditions even suspect the landlord *first*—over friends or family members—when items go missing. Not only is unauthorized entry disrespectful and creepy, it's illegal! An incident like this could end up in court and cost the landlord at least one month's rent and the tenant's attorney fees. Don't make yourself an object of distrust.

Tell me, and I forget; teach me, and I may remember; involve me, and I learn."

—Benjamin Franklin

Day 27: The Dreaded "*S*" Word

You've seen the movies and heard all the jokes. The idea of the "slumlord" is firmly ingrained in popular culture. Local municipal codes have been created to prevent blatant abuses by negligent landlords, such as broken elevators and overflowing garbage. Be aware that there are other legal minimum standards that might not be as obvious, such as providing window screens, having signage for fire escapes, and providing adequate hall and stairway lighting. Periodically reviewing these guidelines is a proactive way to help maintain your property in the best possible condition and to keep the dwelling in compliance. Also, keep in mind that landlords are usually not required to provide major appliances and other such amenities. However, if you do choose to provide stoves, fridges, washers, and dryers, and so forth, it becomes your responsibility to keep that equipment operational.

You are whatever you pretend to be.

Day 28: Maintaining a Safe Property Is the Law

Good landlords have no desire to let a property fall into disrepair. It's good to know minimum standards have been put in place for less responsible landlords, who could give the rest of us a bad name. Tenants have certain legal recourses when landlords don't keep properties up to par. Depending on the area, tenants might have the right to a short-notice termination of the lease agreement, the right to notify an owner of a repair they made and deduct the price from their rent, the right to notify the owner of the need for a repair and withhold rent until it's completed, or even the right to sue an owner for satisfaction of an unresolved repair request. Reasonably maintaining your property is not just good business sense—it's the law.

Success is the sum of small efforts repeated day in and day out.

—Robert Collier

Day 29: BiggerPockets Can Bring You Bigger Pockets

"Life wasn't meant to be lived in a cubicle." How many of us can identify with this slogan from the investor resource BiggerPockets? BiggerPockets is a self-described real estate investing social network, information hub, and marketplace. So it's like a Facebook for landlords—and it's *free*! How cool is that? New and experienced real estate investors join together to help one another become financially free. Instead of a top-down style where the "experts" tell you how things must be done, this resource uses a more grassroots approach. Regular people can connect and express what works and what doesn't work for them. Experienced investors can share wisdom and pick up tips, and those who haven't yet made their first purchase can learn if managing rentals really fits their lifestyle. If two heads are better than one, how about 435,000?

> The slogan "press on" has solved and always will solve the problems of the human race.

Day 30: Nontraditional Routes to Ownership: Getting Your Foot in the Door

Part of what's so exciting about real estate is the variety of routes to opportunities. Many landlords follow nontraditional paths to acquire rental properties. Attend a tax lien or tax deed sale in your area. Tax sales involve properties being sold because the owner fell behind on paying the taxes. Improving real estate markets have decreased the amount of inventory for such sales, but there are still chances to purchase properties at auctions as well. Auctions have helped many new investors afford their first property. Whether you're expanding your real estate portfolio or just starting out on the road to creating a brighter financial future, careful research and planning can lead to great deals at lower prices. Even if you don't make a purchase, attending as a bystander can help you to understand the range of values and types of properties on the market.

Don't stand at the top of the water slide undecided.

Day 31: Taking the Legs Out of Legwork

Developing your investor knowledge is not like the old days, when you learned all you could by calling your realtor and driving all over town to visit open houses. There are tons of online resources begging you to allow them to do a lot of the work for you. Different sites have unique, helpful features. Zillow provides the prices of properties that were recently bought, sold, or rented; square footage; and—everyone's favorite—multiple photos for many residential properties. NeighborhoodScout gives socioeconomic trends and demographic profiles of prospective investing areas. Google Street View will give a virtual view not only of the property itself, but also the surrounding area. Do your research from the comfort of your cozy couch. Then, save the in-person visits—and your gas—only for those properties that meet your high standards.

See the possible—be patient and persistent.

Day 32: "You Mean I Have to Pay for That?" Mandatory Residential Inspections

Different municipalities have different rules for code compliance. Some areas generally require inspections for properties occupied by tenants using rent-subsidy vouchers. Other areas generally require inspections if a code violation is reported or suspected. Other areas practice systematic inspections of all multiple-unit residential housing. These inspections can pose an unexpected cost to new landlords or those coming in from other parts of the country. Find out what inspection fees are associated with owning rental property in your prospective investing area. Also, factor in the cost of your time to meet with the inspector, especially if you invest in a significant number of units. Finally, consider the time it will take for reinspection if a unit doesn't pass on the first round. Don't get caught off guard.

Be all in.

Day 33: Inspections Help Landlords

Some owners dread property inspections, but they can be a great opportunity to comprehensively evaluate the condition of your property. Consider an inspection to be a free assessment by a trained professional to make sure your building is in tip-top shape. Make an inspection as painless as possible by being prepared. Most housing agencies provide a handy checklist to verify that you've resolved all necessary issues in advance. Marking off this list before an inspection saves time for the inspector—and for you, the owner.

Arrive at least one half hour early to do a preinspection walk-through. Discovering that small leak today can help you avoid rotted wood, warped flooring, and moldy drywall tomorrow. Make sure you have all needed keys, and check that you can easily determine which keys open which locks. Being positive and cooperative is good for you in the long run.

Running toward the dream.

Day 34: Why Do We Need Inspections?

Some cities and towns take aggressive measures to minimize substandard, unsanitary, and unsafe residential buildings. Certain areas initiate this process through periodic code-enforcement inspections. The city of Los Angeles, for example, conducts a fresh round of inspections starting every four years. The main reason for safety inspections is to discover illegal units, construction completed without proper permits, and nonpermitted use of existing structures. Other common issues include evidence of rodent and insect infestation, missing or broken smoke and carbon monoxide detectors, damaged electrical fixtures, and blocked access to entrances or exits. Tenants can also submit complaints requesting unscheduled inspections without your knowledge. Always stay one step ahead by making sure your units comply with regulations.

> The miracle isn't that I finished. The miracle is that I had the courage to start.
>
> —John Bingham

Day 35: Don't Allow Untidy Tenants to Put You at Risk

Sometimes tenant actions and behaviors can make a landlord subject to code violations. Uncleanliness of one family can lead to rodents and insects, fire hazards, and other issues that affect the landlord and all residents of a particular building. First, make sure you're communicating expectations to all incoming residents. Next, post these friendly expectations in a common area. If necessary, exercise your right to get rid of problem tenants who refuse to comply. A dirty unit is a lease violation. Many standard leases contain a clause similar to the following: "Tenant shall maintain the premises in a clean, presentable, and safe condition at all times and in accordance with all health, safety, and building-code regulations." Don't let one untidy tenant put you at risk or lower the quality of living standards that you work hard to maintain for your other residents.

Compete with yourself, not with others.

Day 36: Licensed to Be a Landlord: Understanding Licensing and Registration

Licensed to drive. Licensed to hunt. Licensed to fish. Why not "licensed to landlord"? In many places, such as Washington, DC, and Philadelphia, residential units must be registered annually with the municipality. Fees for what are called Certificates of Occupancy or Certificates of Residential Suitability can run from fifty to one hundred dollars or more. In places like Schaumburg, Illinois, landlords must attend a mandatory class on crime prevention in addition to becoming registered and scheduling annual inspections for all rental property. These guidelines apply to all leased, commercial, or rented property. Some areas require landlords to notify the municipality even if the family living in a unit is not paying rent. Forms such as the Family Living in Unit acknowledgment help local governments keep track of which properties are occupied in their town. Factor in these costs when determining your rents.

Strive for progress, not perfection.

Day 37: Party with a Purpose: Building Community among Your Residents

One low-cost method any landlord can use to reduce headaches throughout the year is to organize an annual cookout at each rental property. Tenants can get to know one another and get to see you in a more casual setting. Sponsor the bulk of the food items, and residents can showcase their signature dishes. Facilitate icebreakers and family-style games. You might be surprised at how little people know about a neighbor who has occupied the same space for years. Your real goal is not social but instead business. You're not looking to build an army of BFFs. If you introduce tenants to one another, you make them feel more comfortable to approach their neighbors when issues arise (noise disturbances, misplaced mail, parking issues, etc.) instead of calling you first.

You only lose what you cling to.

—Buddha

Day 38: Aim for Fairness, Not Kindness

When it comes to extending courtesies to tenants, many landlords struggle with where to draw the line. Sometimes a tenant's troubles might draw on your heartstrings and cause you to make exceptions to your business practices. But it's no secret that kindness is not always appreciated. That's why your goal as a landlord is not to aim for kindness, but to aim for fairness. Life happens, even to tenants. But don't let their problems become your problems. Although it's true that fairness is not always rewarded, at least being fair puts you in a less vulnerable position and avoids leaving you feeling like you gave more than you should. Others look out for their own self-interests. You have to look out for yours, too. Even when things don't go as planned, you can sleep better at night.

The dream is free, but the hustle is sold separately.

Day 39: Don't Kick the Can down the Road

One of the biggest mistakes new and experienced landlords make is putting off eviction while waiting for a situation to improve. Some drag their feet on evicting a tenant and accept excuse after excuse. Be realistic when a tenant consistently falls behind on rent payments. A life change (or even just poor money management) could affect the tenant's ability to afford your unit. Address a problem that is not likely to get better, and do it sooner rather than later. Allowing a tenant to build up a big balance that he or she can't pay is not really doing the tenant any favors, either. Big balances can make tenants do desperate things and force you to have to ding their credit by taking them to court. Don't kick the can down the road and delay the inevitable.

Progress is impossible without change, and those who cannot change their minds cannot change anything.

Day 40: Don't Let Tenants' Actions Make You So Poor That You Can't Run Your Business

Your dream is to own beautiful, well-maintained properties while exceeding the expectations of well-paying tenants. Every month you find you fall short of your own expectations because you don't take in enough funds to cover your projected costs. Instead of full, on-time rent payments, a few bad apples only offer you repeated excuses and promises. The condition of your property is affected, and the good tenants suffer as well. Problems like this can spread like a disease. If one tenant with a good payment record hears that another slow-paying tenant has not faced any real consequences, the tenant who pays on time can become resentful and start testing the boundaries as well. Very soon you'll find your resources stretched so thin that you can't make good choices for your investment. Remember: the power to put a stop to late payments lies with you.

What is the point of being alive if you don't at least try to do something remarkable?

Day 41: Knowing Your Property's Worth

"Know your worth!" This time-tested advice has been offered to job seekers and people on the dating scene for ages. We apply this standard to honoring our own personal value. We should also apply it to our quality rental units. Maintain an intimate knowledge of market rental prices in your area. Know how you rate compared with similar units, and set rents accordingly. Trulia, RentBits, Rentometer, Zillow, City-Data.com, Craigslist, and other free sites offer a wealth of data. Don't be afraid to gather info the old-fashioned way as well. Call the owners of properties for sale, check classified sections of local papers, or call your real estate agent for comparisons. Don't undervalue (or overvalue) your rentals. Not only should you recognize the level of quality you offer, but make sure that level is clear to whoever is lucky enough to benefit from it.

*You must give everything to make your life as beautiful
as the dreams that dance in your imagination.*

Day 42: What Is *Section 8*, and What Does It Mean to Me?

Section 8 is the common nickname for the eighth section of the US Housing Act of 1937. The official name is the Housing Choice Voucher Program. This federally funded program provides rent subsidies for preapproved renters in the private market. It helps make market rents affordable to more vulnerable members of society (elderly or disabled renters and low-income families). Benefits to landlords include a larger tenant pool, prompt payments, and the hope that tenants will be on their best behavior to maintain their vouchers. Landlords who rent to voucher holders receive a major portion of the tenant's rent directly from the government. In exchange, landlords agree to adhere to program guidelines for providing safe, sanitary, and decent housing. Some landlords view the regular inspections, government oversight, and limitations on how much rent can be charged as drawbacks.

If it's to be...it's up to me.

Day 43: "Minimum Housing Quality Standards," You Say...Aren't They Obvious?

We all have our standards. We would like to believe that no landlord needs to be told that a rental must have a kitchen and at least one working bathroom. Historical abuses in the residential rental industry, however, led to government intervention in the form of housing laws. Housing inspectors with the Section 8 voucher program use a uniform code of Housing Quality Standards (HQS), developed by the Department of Housing and Urban Development (HUD). These codes cover everything from the foundation to the ventilation, entry locks, natural light requirements, and even the condition of the roof. The sad reality is that a great deal of substandard housing still exists today. HQS guidelines at least provide a clear set of minimum expectations for renters who seek remedies for negligent owners.

We cannot cure the world of sorrows, but we can choose to live in joy.

Day 44: The Tenant Is Your Teammate for Section 8 Inspections

Tenants often have as much of a desire to pass the inspection as the owner. Happy tenants work to minimize disruptions from this annual event. Work with tenants to make the process run smoothly. Tenants are notified by mail of pending inspections, but touch base with them to make sure they're aware. You can even provide a copy of the minimum housing-standards guidelines to all new residents, so they'll know what to look for. Encourage tenants to notify you of inspections as far in advance as possible, so you have enough time to address maintenance and repair issues. Finally, remind the tenant to make sure the unit and common areas are clean and orderly when the big day comes. It's your job (and to your benefit) to help the tenant understand that passing inspections during the first round is everyone's goal.

It's not who you are that holds you back; it's who you think you're not.

Day 45: Determining Your Comprehensive Marketing Budget

Direct-mail marketing will probably be a major piece in your marketing puzzle, but don't limit yourself. Mail campaigns are part of your marketing budget, but they're only one part. The more creative you are in your efforts to reach people, the more likely you are to get positive attention. Remember that networking is also key to your marketing plan. One benefit of networking is that it usually doesn't cost very much—some business cards and maybe the cost of attending some workshops and seminars. Although networking has a low monetary cost, it does require an investment of your time. Factor in the opportunity cost of the time spent networking, which takes you away from activities that can directly generate income. Make sure the "free time" you use for networking is applied to activities that will produce the best return on your investment.

> The greatest prison that people live in is the fear of what other people think.

Day 46: Don't Make the Same Mistakes

Here are a few mistakes that real estate owners have confessed to and that you can avoid. Be prepared for tax hikes. Taxes can go up suddenly, and if you have not calculated your rent price accordingly, you may find yourself taking a loss. So it is always better to keep a buffer while calculating your rent.

Tenants can cost you a lot of damage if you do not watch out. Tenants do not own the house—you do. Tenants are not going to make a profit or a loss—you are. So be prepared for damage that your tenants can do to your property. A lot of damage can happen in a short amount of time if you allow it to, and the only way to prevent it is to visit your properties frequently. Good tenants are worth their weight in gold. The corollary to this statement is that if you find good tenants, keep them close to you, even if it means a lower rent. Remember that whatever you lose in rent, you gain by saving on the cost of repairs.

Repairs will be expensive and unexpected. Repairs occur at the wrong time and can cost a lot. Always set aside a contingency fund to take care of this. A small part of your profit should always be set aside for repairs, to lessen future heartaches. Set out all the rules you want to be followed in the lease and stick to them. Live by the rules you have set out. Let tenants know that the rules matter and that there are consequences for late rent payments, damages, and other infractions. Being a landlord is not for the faint of heart; it is both risky and rewarding. If done right, it offers good profits and financial freedom. Just remember to learn from your mistakes and those of other landlords.

Every accomplishment starts with the decision to try.

Day 47: The Best Time

The market is always dependent on timing. Be it the stock market, digital technology, or news, timing is of the essence. Is there some kind of timing secret for the real estate market as well? Yes and no. Because housing is a necessity and not a luxury, houses are constantly being sold. But your timing may determine the rates and views you get for your property. Spring and fall are buying seasons; there is an increase in home inventory during spring and fall, which means more options for buyers. So if you want to get a good deal while selling, try it during "off" seasons, such as winter and holiday seasons. This way you may target "desperate" buyers in need of a home when there is little inventory. The first Sunday open house is the holy grail of real estate. Most agents and sellers try to hit the listings on late Thursday to Friday morning, with Sunday being the first showing. Get more views by listing on Monday or Tuesday and build up momentum to have a strong opening on Sunday. Learn your market, talk to the agents, and find the patterns.

Never meet expectations. Exceed them.

Day 48: "Hi, Jake. Yes, It's Me Again!" The Right Insurance for Your Situation

Do you file so many insurance claims that Jake from Some Farm Insurance has you first on his speed dial? Or does your insurance agent ask when you call, perhaps every ten years or so, "Who's calling, please? Oh, I see. Can I call you back in half an hour after I grab your file from basement storage?" Most areas of the country require property owners to carry some type of basic insurance. However, not all owners have the same level and types of insurance needs. If you own property in a high-crime area that is also prone to natural disasters, you likely need more insurance. If your property is in an area rarely affected by extreme forces of nature or criminal damage, your needs might be lower. Also consider these factors in deciding your deductible.

Tough times don't last, but tough people do.

Day 49: Dearest Home Insurance, How Can I Save on Thee? Let Me Count the Ways...

Are you paying more than you should for insurance? There are some things you can do to make sure you're getting the best value. Review your policy once a year, usually just before renewal. Remember that longevity can have rewards. Check with your current provider to see if they offer loyalty discounts for longtime customers or those with multiple policies. Also, take this opportunity to shop around. You might get a better deal somewhere else as a new customer. Make your agent aware of any steps you've taken to make it less likely that you'll need to file a claim, such as adding a security system, making the building more fire resistant, or implementing a "no pets" policy. Have the value of your property reassessed. Market conditions might have decreased what your property is worth; your insurance rate should reflect this accordingly.

Strong people don't put others down—they lift them up.

Day 50: "Sure, Honey. I'll Just Run Downstairs to Grab a Flashlight—Arrrrrghhhh!"

A storm rages outside. You lose power and go to the basement to grab a flashlight. Not only are you in the dark, but you now discover you're ankle deep in murky water. These costly, private nightmares happen every day in buildings across the country. Yucky water in my basement is yucky water in my basement, right? Wrong. Not all water catastrophes are created equally. Water entering a building over or through a breach in the foundation is considered flooding. If you live in a low-lying area, ask your insurance agent about flood insurance. In older cities, antiquated sewer systems are notorious for water that backs up through sewer drains, sump pumps, and toilets. Ask your agent about water and sump-pump backup coverage. Knowing the difference between types of disasters is important for determining what steps are needed in order to protect yourself.

*When we seek to discover the best in others, we
somehow bring out the best in ourselves.*

Day 51: Raindrops Keep Falling on My Head

Just because you don't have old pots sitting around to catch the drips doesn't mean it's not time to replace that old roof. Before you call a roofer, use these easy self-assessments to know how much time you have left. Determine the age of your roof. New roofs generally last up to twenty-five years. Did the most recent job involve a second layer of shingles applied over the first, or was there a complete tear-off? Curling or buckling shows where the heat of the sun has taken a shingle past its useful life. If you see daylight through the boards of the attic, *run*—don't walk—to contact a trusted professional for an immediate estimate. Any of these issues on a roof that is only a few years old might mean that it was installed improperly. Are you eligible for reimbursement?

Today I will do what others won't, so tomorrow I can accomplish what others can't.

Day 52: Putting Out the No Vacancy Sign for Pests

Certain hospitalities can make a property attractive to rodents and insects. After a long, hard day of running around and spreading their general nastiness all over, there's nothing pests like more than a refreshing drink of H_2O. Make sure to drain all standing water around the grounds of your property. Exterminate regularly. If you wait until you see a problem, it might be more advanced than you realize. Seal up all cracks and holes on the exterior and interior of the property. Get tenants involved in keeping a property pest-free. Remind them to dispose of trash properly and to keep yards free of clutter and possible nesting areas. While it's impossible for a building owner to guarantee that property will never be visited by unwanted guests, don't roll out the red carpet.

Live in the sunshine. Swim in the sea. Drink the wild air.

Day 53: Open Carry, Concealed Carry, or Neither?

Are you liable if someone is injured on your property by the gun of a licensed owner? What happens if a tragedy at one of your buildings could have been prevented if a resident had access to a handgun? Do you know the difference between *open carry* and *concealed carry*? Not so long ago, nonenthusiasts hardly gave a second thought to gun laws, unless they lived in a big hunting community or a high-crime area. With Texas at the forefront of the discussion, increasing incidents involving guns have raised public debate in communities across the country. Heightened interest leads to more legislation. We see the universal No Gun sign with a red circle and a slash over the image of a gun being posted in some areas, whereas more gun-friendly signs are going up in others. Learn how local gun laws apply to your rentals.

What if I fall? Oh, but, my darling, what if you fly?

Day 54: You Said the Check Was in the Mail a Week Ago!

Accepting personal checks for rent payments can be an act of faith. First, there's no guarantee that a check was actually sent. If you do receive it, how long before retraced funds from a bounced check prove it's no more than a picture of cute kittens frolicking? Ahhh, so adorable—and so useless. ACH, or Automated Clearing House, payments are electronic transfers of money. They were originally used for direct deposits of employee paychecks, but the benefits have increased popularity for other types of transactions. It can take weeks for the funds on a personal check to fully clear, but ACH payments usually take only three days. ACH rent-collection services, such as Secure Pay One, even offer these services free to tenants. These payments are not only more efficient and more convenient for your tenants, they're also safer and less expensive for you.

Remember how far you've come, not just how far you have to go. You are not where you want to be, but neither are you where you used to be.

Day 55: Class B Apartments: Affordable Housing for Working-Class Renters

A harsh reality is that owning a home won't be everyone's American dream. For many, financial limitations put the prospect so out of reach that this option will never be available. A subset of the housing industry caters to perpetual renters, or what some call "renters by necessity," rather than "renters by choice." Class B apartments are market-rate units with few amenities. They're designed to be workforce housing for so-called gray- or blue-collar workers. Because these renters are more sensitive to price, investors are careful not to overimprove units. The typical rehab cost for a Class B unit is $10,000 versus the average $30,000 per Class A unit. Deep-pocketed entities, such as pension funds, dominate Class A rental investing. However, the Class B market is becoming increasingly more competitive as many independent entrepreneurs step into the fray.

Change your thoughts, and you can change the world.

Day 56: What Does That HOA Membership Really Cost?

You just invested in a beautiful condo in a charming, well-established part of town. This stately, historical building has a lot of charm and character. You can't believe how low the assessments are—what a great deal! Then the elevator breaks down, and the thirty-year-old roof springs several leaks. You don't find out until then that the homeowner association (HOA) board is down to $206 in the reserve account for emergencies. The HOA board approves a huge special assessment; you watch your monthly dues quadruple—and your rental profits disappear.

Annual HOA fees are used to maintain the common areas and the building. Major expenses can result in additional charges, running up to thousands of dollars. Always ask how often fines increase and by how much, how fee increases are set, how large the reserve fund is, and so forth.

Open your mouth only if what you are going to say is more beautiful than silence.

Day 57: Who's in Charge Here? The Importance of Knowing Who Manages Your HOA

The typical image of an HOA in popular culture is a hyperwatchful, overbearing Big Brother organization, writing letters and applying harsh fines for the smallest violations. Neighbors spy on neighbors to make sure everyone plants the right color of rose bush. This can happen when an HOA is managed by a professional company and residents volunteer to serve on the HOA board. Keep in mind that some HOAs live at the other end of the spectrum, and undermanagement of an HOA can be a bigger problem. When HOA reps don't care enough about maintenance, making repairs, serving on the board, or hearing grievances, the quality of life in the whole building declines. Some HOAs even randomly appoint residents to be president, like it or not. Who knows—your turn might be next in the captain's seat. Before you invest, know who manages the HOA.

People inspire you, or they drain you. Pick them wisely.

Day 58: The Good Book Says to Care for Widows and Orphans

Never underestimate the power of an HOA or take for granted the possibility of legal recourse, including foreclosure. One couple living in a Florida retirement community fought their HOA after it objected to them taking custody of their six-year-old granddaughter. Their daughter, the child's mother, was ruled unfit to parent due to a drug addiction. The HOA board said the child didn't meet the over fifty-five residency restriction. The couple was forced to sell their home at a loss. Another HOA sued to halt the reconstruction of a unit destroyed by a plane crash. Even though the unimaginable tragedy claimed the life of the owner's wife and his infant son, the board objected to the type of shingles the owner chose for reconstruction. The HOA won the case. For an investor who appreciates the ability to cut corners, HOAs can pose insurmountable obstacles.

> Worrying won't stop the bad stuff from happening; it just stops you from enjoying the good.

Day 59: The Politics of HOA Management

Sure, she baked cookies for your son when he won his first soccer game. But the old adage "Power corrupts" could even apply to sweet little Mrs. Higginbottom in 3B, once she gets that HOA gavel in her hand. By definition, HOAs are made up of regular people living in close proximity. Conflict is to be expected, but sometimes petty politics and power trips rise to epic proportions. How does this HOA resolve conflicts? Has it ever had to sue a resident? If so, what was the outcome? Sit in on an HOA meeting or at least try to get copies of the last several meetings. Talk to HOA members who aren't on the board, if possible, for an objective viewpoint. Find out the current and past conflicts. Does this HOA display an unhealthy level of drama? Is it worth the trouble to buy here?

Life is either a daring adventure or nothing.

Day 60: It's Not Just Whether an HOA Is Right for You—Are You Right for the HOA?

The HOA board forces the crazy cat lady to limit the size of her wandering brood. Residents are quick to do a little dance. People are usually *less* enthusiastic when policies are directed toward themselves. Many of the same qualities that make these types of residences attractive to owners and renters are viewed through a different lens when HOA members are confronted by policy limits. What was attractive *uniformity* becomes restrictive *conformity*. The major rewards of owning property include being king or queen of your castle and having the option to customize it to your needs. Assess your own temperament before investing in an HOA community. If you are the type of investor who hates being told what to do, HOA rules could lead to frustration for you. Carefully consider how this arrangement fits your lifestyle.

Our lives are defined by opportunities, even the ones we miss.

Day 61: Don't Make Lemonade by Buying Someone Else's Lemons

The owner of a lovely three-bedroom condo is selling you on all the wonderful features of his or her unit. You sense that the owner accidentally revealed that he or she has only been there for four months. The owner glosses over that fact, explaining that he or she got a great new job on the other side of town—so he or she tells you. The owner fails to mention that the HOA is suing him or her for the large unauthorized "improvement" he or she made to the unit, causing him or her to rack up daily fines. Inheriting someone else's problem can be a major headache. Do your research in advance to make sure the property you want to buy meets all policy guidelines. Owners do have the option to appeal to the HOA board for permission to bend rules, but successful variance requests are not common for HOA communities. Caveat emptor—buyer beware.

You are confined only by the walls you build yourself.

Day 62: Some Restrictions Apply: How HOA Rules Affect the Investors

Condos, townhouses, gated communities, and other planned-development residences are often subject to HOAs. Membership is usually mandatory and involves certain rules, called covenants, conditions, and restrictions (CC&Rs), that all residents must follow. Review the CC&Rs online. Verify that the info is current. Find out the consequences if you violate a rule. One common HOA rule prevents the display of lawn signs. Although this provides a welcome reprieve from an unsightly sea of Reelect Mayor Wilkins signs, how does this limit you as an investor when you're trying to sell? The biggest CC&R affecting investors, by far, is whether or not this HOA will even allow you to rent out the unit. Is this community restricted to owner-occupants? This is a huge question for a landlord. Make sure you know the answer before you take the next step.

Sometimes the smallest step in the right direction ends up being the biggest step of your life. Tiptoe if you must, but take the step.

Day 63: I'm on Board with That HOA Rule, but What about My Tenant?

Thinking about renting to a supermodel or an exotic dancer? See if your HOA prohibits the wearing of high-heel shoes indoors, like one HOA board in New York that does. That prospective applicant plumber passed the credit check with flying colors? Remember, your HOA prohibits visible parking of commercial vehicles—your building better have a garage. Each area has its own rental laws, with HOA rules on top of those. Then, the renter is accountable to the owner, who is accountable to the HOA board. Complications arise when layers of rules are applied to layers of people. If your tenant repeatedly breaks the rules, will the HOA hold *you* responsible? You can't discriminate against certain renters based on potential HOA issues, but you can cover yourself. Clearly share expectations with potential renters. Allow the applicants to decide if this is the right community for them.

The secret of change is to focus all your energy not on fighting the old, but on building the new.

Day 64: Do Your Tenants Suffer from "HOA Syndrome"?

Do your tenants lie awake at night, wondering if they'll wake to find that their cars have been ticketed or towed? Do they have a fear of going to the mailbox, losing a pet, or allowing their children to play in front of their home? University of Southern Nevada psychiatrist Dr. Gary Solomon has developed a diagnosis of what he calls "HOA Syndrome," a type of anxiety similar to post-traumatic stress disorder. Other symptoms include depression, sadness, hypervigilance, constant anger, irritability, wakefulness, and paranoia. If dealing with HOA politics is causing you or your tenants real mental stress, consider selling the property and investing in another community. No amount of profit you earn on any investment is worth compromising your physical and mental well-being.

You can, you should, and if you're brave enough to start, you will.

Day 65: What Is This Wholesaling Thing We Hear So Much about These Days?

The practice of wholesaling has been around forever but is getting so popular that it's become a household word. The process involves an investor who very briefly buys or even just gets a property under contract and then sells or assigns the contract as quickly as possible. The wholesaler finds the property at the lowest possible price and then makes it available to the second investor, who will then fix up the property, either to rent it out or to flip it. One of the biggest advantages of wholesaling is that a skilled investor can get into the business with little or no money to start. Time, motivation, and legwork can be substituted for capital in this investment strategy. Wholesaling can be a gateway for the novice real estate entrepreneur whose biggest hurdle is acquiring enough funds to get started.

Running teaches us to keep moving forward, one step at a time, especially in the most painful moments.

Day 66: Beyond the Multiple Listing Service: How to Find Properties to Wholesale

The key to wholesaling is not just finding inexpensive properties. You have to find properties at a price low enough to leave room to include your finder's fee. Finding a property with a price low enough to wholesale on the Multiple Listing Service (MLS) is not impossible, but it's unlikely. There are many better ways to track them down. Many investors claim the best way to bring business to you is through an ongoing and consistent direct-mail campaign to absentee owners. You can attend REIA meetings, use websites that feature off-market properties, or talk to the neighbors of a long-abandoned property. Advertise through billboards or place a sign on your car. All you need is a little creativity and willingness to put in the legwork.

*Attract what you expect, reflect what you desire,
become what you respect, and mirror what you admire.*

Day 67: Don't Be Penny-Wise and Pound-Foolish: Following Rental Registration Guidelines

"Not *another* expense!" Some landlords gripe about the process of rental registration that exists in many areas, such as Seattle, Washington. Rental-unit registration makes it possible for the city to find owners in case of emergencies. Registration also ensures that cities or towns can keep owners informed of and accountable for adhering to building codes and maintaining safe housing. Fees are usually a modest amount to cover the city's cost to send out notices and maintain a database. Some landlords prefer to cut corners and bypass this process. Beware: penalties for not complying with the red tape can far outweigh the costs. Failure to adhere to requirements can subject you to fines around ten times the price of the license or more—even for your first offense. Understand the consequences of not knowing or breaking the local rules.

In the end, we only regret the chances we didn't take.

Day 68: Occupancy Rates Rise, and Occupancy Rates Fall

Some landlords in hard-hit recovering areas grudgingly hold on to problem tenants, not realizing their market is on the rise. Other landlords experience long vacancies, holding out for high rents no longer supported by formerly hot areas that have started to cool. It's the eternal cycle of the rental industry. Watching national numbers can provide big-picture insight. A well-informed Texas landlord, for example, might be interested in following broad trends. Keep in mind that these numbers will include what's happening in the Las Vegas, Florida, and New York rental markets, and remember that important real estate trends can be strictly local. Very different factors can even affect neighborhoods on opposite sides of the same town. Never strictly depend on national numbers. Keep an eye on a variety of factors, including unemployment, population growth, occupancy, and new construction rates in *your* area—regardless of good times or bad.

Good things are going to happen.

Day 69: A Space to Call Your Own

Sure, you're proud of your child's progress in her architectural model-building class. And your mate's first batch from his craft-beer kit is coming along quite nicely. But where is the clear surface in your home to use to manage your rentals? If you're starting out as an investor, it's crucial to have a dedicated space to conduct business and keep track of important paperwork. Minimum amenities should include a computer with Microsoft Office, a printer, a high-quality digital camera (your smartphone's camera should work just fine), and a calculator to add up your loads of rental income. If you can't designate an exclusive space, make it as easy as possible to set up and take down your office. In this way, taking advantage of unexpected blocks of free time by "stepping into your office" won't feel like a chore.

I can, and I will.

Day 70: Keeping Your Spirits Up

Preparing your mind for the game of real estate investing is not just about education. It also involves developing a positive mental outlook. Television shows and seminars, such as those given by local real estate gurus passing through your area, can give a false impression that managing rentals takes zero effort. Being a successful landlord is rarely just a weekend hobby. The game can get tough at times. Make time to read books by motivational experts like David Bach, Suze Orman, Robert Kiyosaki, Napoleon Hill, and Zig Ziglar. If you just can't find the time to sit down and read, listen to these authors on audiobook while you perform other tasks, such as maintenance and repairs on your rental property. Consistently starting each day with as little as ten to thirty minutes of self-development builds up your armor to face potential challenges.

> Strength doesn't come from what you can do. It comes from overcoming the things you once thought you couldn't.

Day 71: Discovering Why You Invest: What Kind of Life Do You Want?

The beauty of real estate investing is that there are so many paths to financial security. If you implement any sound strategy, the money will come. So the question is not, "Can I make money in real estate?" The real question is, "What is the way to make money in real estate that best suits my lifestyle and my personality?" Start by asking yourself why you're investing. What are your talents, goals, desires, and passions?

Do you desire to show your creative side by arranging sweet deals the average investor wouldn't see? You might be drawn to a hands-on strategy that involves a lot of oversight. Or are you the type of investor who wants to "fix it and forget it"? Selecting a sustainable investment strategy is not just about your balance sheet. Seek a strategy that brings you the biggest emotional returns.

Human beings, by changing the inner beliefs of their minds, can change the outer aspects of their lives.

Day 72: What's Your Brand?

Do you specialize, or is your real estate expertise of a more general nature? How do you want to be recognized? What's the first thing you want people in the business to remember when they hear your name? Your first step is to figure out what you have to offer. Spend a little time developing your professional identity. Once you have a clear sense of the niche you fill in the market, you can strategically begin to build your personal brand. Now the fun part: hire professionals to create a logo and tag line for your business cards, website, and marketing campaign. You're ready to go! Whether you decide to work solo or to join with a group of other investors, presenting a strong personal brand can bring you amazing returns on your investment.

> Don't focus on your weaknesses; focus on your strengths.

Day 73: Only Knowledge *in Action* Is Power

People are often confused by the real meaning behind that old saying "Knowledge is power." The "power" is only released when that knowledge is *applied*. Acquiring the knowledge is only the first step. It helps to have a focus on the type of information you seek. In Napoleon Hill's book *Think and Grow Rich*, Hill advocates for seeking specialized knowledge. He believes that the only way for knowledge to have power—which in his case refers to the power to attract money—is if it is organized and intelligently directed. He went on to write that millions of people have misinterpreted this idea by treating it as a one-step process. Hill recommends setting up practical plans of action and following through with those plans to achieve a definite end. In the case of investing, that "end" is usually financial freedom.

There's always a person who'll appreciate whoever you are and ride the rollercoaster with you.

Day 74: I Found the Perfect Investment Today! Now, Where Did I Put That Address?

Was that the three-bedroom/two-bath on Fleetwood Drive, next to the house with the chicken coop in the yard? Or was that the two-bedroom/one-bath on Archway Lane? Sooner or later the details of your prospects will become a jumble in your head. Developing a system is an obvious idea. The problem is that we get so excited starting out but then fail to think of it until we are staring at a loosely organized pile of information.
Addresses and phone numbers scribbled on fast-food napkins won't do the trick. Consider setting up an Excel spreadsheet with columns for property address, features, contact number, how you found it, and any additional notes. Don't wait until your business gets going at a healthy clip to focus on keeping track of all your great opportunities (or the ones you want to avoid).

My health, my wealth.

Day 75: Helping Your Tenants Helps You More

Sometimes landlords and property managers lag behind tenant expectations for convenience. Owners might be deterred by the cost of implementing certain technologies. Sometimes it's just a matter of relying on old habits. There are times when owners can benefit from a nudge from tenants in the direction of progress. One survey, for example, shows that a majority of residents welcome the convenience of paying rent online. Only roughly a quarter of owners, however, make this option available to residents. Consider how making certain things easier for your tenants can benefit *you* even more in the long run. Online payments help to minimize late-payment excuses because the check won't be "lost in the mail." It even saves trees by moving away from a paper-based system. The advantages outweigh the costs—ultimately creating a better situation for both the landlord and tenant.

Although the brave may not live forever, the cautious do not live at all.

Day 76: Tenant Tom's Happy Birthday

Tenant Tom was uneasy. His fiftieth-birthday wine-tasting/BBQ bash was set for Saturday, but his air conditioner broke down on Wednesday. It was July. Your HVAC guy checked it out but found he needed to order a replacement part. On Friday morning, your tenant received a text message at the office from your fancy digital work-order system. Your contractor installed the part just after the tenant left for work. Tom breathes a sigh of relief. He shakes his head, remembering the last building he lived in. He never knew if a request was completed until he walked in the door. Calls to the management company to check the status only went to voice mail. Digital work-order systems help management staff quickly and easily communicate with residents. Residents feel less frustrated about planning around service requests if they receive regular status updates.

Positivity is the key to your happiness.

Day 77: "I'm So Glad I Found You!" Buyers and Sellers Come Together for Lease Options

Picture two couples. The expectant buyers with bruised credit trudge up a hill, looking for banks willing to loosen their purse strings in a tight credit market. Meanwhile, the anxious sellers, forced to put their lives on hold because they can't sell their home, climb the other side. These two families meet up at the summit and negotiate a happy compromise—the lease option, or rent to own. The buyers can "try before they buy," gaining interest in a property without the big down payment. The sellers can cover their mortgage and buy time until the sale of the property. One of the downsides for sellers includes buyers who walk away at the end of the term without exercising their option to buy. Buyers risk locking in a set price, even if values fall, or being scammed by sellers who are in foreclosure.

Never look back—that is not the direction you are heading.

Day 78: Landlord Business Hours

The tenant in 1B calls at 1:00 a.m. to say he's locked out of his apartment. Again. Gee whiz—that's the third time this year. Wouldn't it be nice if there was a type of property where you could flip your landlord Open sign over to Closed? Actually, there is. One of the major appeals of owning commercial property rather than rental property involves the limited hours of operation. Residential renters are known for expressing their needs 24-7, 365 days a year, but business tenants in commercial properties often limit their activity to business hours. I guess that's where they get the name. Business tenants have much less reason—or expectation—for the landlord to be on constant standby. Even in urgent situations, such as fires or break-ins, the owner can rest easy, knowing that the alarm company is ready to notify emergency personnel right away.

Let it be enough.

Day 79: "I'll Take a Large Order of Industrial with a Side of Retail"

Residential real estate investing is usually the first choice for people just starting out. More and more investors, however, are choosing to sample the larger smorgasbord. The term *commercial property* is applied to most types of structures that are not strictly used for residential purposes. It includes industrial, retail/restaurant, and office buildings. Miscellaneous nonresidential buildings, such as hotels, hospitals, and self-storage facilities, fall into this category. Some states also classify multiple-family buildings with more than four units as commercial. *Mixed-use properties* house a mix of types, such as retail, office, and apartments. The broader term *commercial real estate* expands to include vacant or undeveloped land. With so many different and wonderful ways to generate greater revenue than just collecting rent for a living space, it's no wonder so many entrepreneurs are drawn to the appeal of investing in commercial property.

Everything happens for a reason.

Day 80: Team Commercial or Team Residential: Which One to Choose?

Some landlords are squarely in the camp of residential-property investing. They talk about the lower buy-in costs, fewer public safety concerns, less maintenance due to lower traffic, and less need for a professional manager. Some landlords swear by the virtues of commercial real estate. They cite more objective price evaluations, flexible lease terms, and lessees who might pay all the expenses except the mortgage. Then there are the owners who happily live with a foot in each world by investing in a hybrid—mixed-use buildings. All three types of owners can present strong cases for why their choice is best. The beauty of real estate lies in the fact that you don't have to choose between options. You can build your portfolio with one or the other or all three. It is possible to win big with any combination!

Give yourself the 100 percent chance to succeed, or you won't.

Day 81: Call Now! Operators Are Standing By

Are you a commercial property owner whose property taxes eat up more than 20 percent of your gross rents? Have you been affected by unusually high vacancy rates? Have changes in market forces or building and community conditions taken a toll on the revenue being generated by your property? Help is available. Seeking professional or legal assistance can possibly lead to a refund of, or at least a reduction in, assessed values, or even savings on current and future tax bills. The cost of this service usually amounts to a percentage of the estimated savings to the owner. Be aware that savings are not likely to be permanent, and the appeal might need to be resubmitted periodically to coincide with local tax-reassessment cycles. Act now—don't wait! You might be entitled to real relief, and this is no infomercial.

The biggest obstacles we face in life are the limits we place on ourselves.

Day 82: "Your References Are in Order, Sparky, but Tell Me Why You Left Your Last Position"

Yes, indeed. Pet references do exist, and they're becoming more common as rates of pet ownership rise. Ask the previous landlord for clues about the pet's personality, in the same way you ask for an impression of the tenant. Another way to assess your exposure to pet issues in advance is through a visit to the prospective tenant's home. Pay special attention to larger animals, untrained or hyperactive pets, multiple-pet families, and older pets. Some landlords charge higher rents for bigger dogs, which generally cause greater damage, or multiple dogs, whose aggressive play can lead to accidents. Unsuspecting landlords might choose cats over dogs. Cats are often perceived to be more self-sufficient and less destructive. Be aware that cat urine can be much stronger and longer lasting. The smell of an unkempt home occupied by cats can be detected from fifty feet away.

I can do anything. It's a simple phrase, but it helps to remind yourself—you really can do anything you set your mind to.

Day 83: Is a Landlord Ever Responsible for a Tenant's Pet?

Renting to families with pets increases the applicant pool. Owners can also charge higher rents and additional security deposits. There are risks, however, that some owners feel outweigh the benefits. Certain cities have ordinances against particular types of dogs. This can be a double-edged sword. Although it takes the pressure off owners for prohibiting aggressive breeds, it can result in a landlord liability if the pet is knowingly allowed to live in the unit and it harms a person or another animal. Some landlords prefer to avoid families with pets completely. If you choose this route, how can you make sure residents stick to your rules? Adding a fee in your leases for each sighting of an unauthorized pet sends a clear message. Checking for signs of pets during regular inspections can root out rule breakers.

Don't let life discourage you; everyone who got where he or she is had to begin where he or she was.

Day 84: Dogs and Small Apartments

Dogs can thrive in small rentals if special care is taken by their owners. Many are content with a little exercise twice a day and an energetic workout once a week. Regular contact with other dogs helps keep them in good spirits. Consistent schedules are physically and mentally reassuring to a pet. A well-trained puppy finds it easier to understand the rules of the house and become less disruptive. Finally, Mr. Pickles needs to have his own space—even in a unit as small as a studio. A little corner is fine. Ironically, the size of the breed is not always an accurate indicator. Huge, laid-back dogs such as Great Danes can fare better in cozy spaces than small, high-energy breeds like terriers. Consider adjusting your policy for breeds of any size where research shows they do well in apartment settings.

> I am grateful for all my problems. After each one was overcome, I became stronger and more able to meet those that were still to come. I grew in all my difficulties.

Day 85: Making It Easier to Change Your "No-Dogs" Policy

Many landlords are tapping into the growing pool of renters who are a part of dog-owning families, whereas some prefer to lag behind the trend. These owners are unsure if dogs and apartments are a good mix. Are you a landlord considering changing your "no-pets" policy? Don't continue to watch your pool of nonpet applicants shrink without thinking about giving Sparky a chance. Interview potential applicants. Ask general, open-ended, noninvasive questions about their relationships with their pets. Answers may reveal if their pets are adjusted to multifamily living. Share a handout on tips for keeping dogs content in rental units with new tenants upon move in. This way, they won't feel defensive that you're singling out their precious pets. They might even appreciate that you care enough to help their pets feel more comfortable.

I'm too busy working on my own grass to notice if yours is greener.

Day 86: Pet Deposits versus Per-Pet Rent Increases

Many landlords opt to charge tenants a deposit for the privilege of allowing pets to live in the unit. Consider that a one-time deposit might only go so far. The cost of removing deeply ingrained pet odors when a tenant moves out might greatly exceed the amount of the deposit—especially if a tenant lives in your unit for several years. You can instead see if your area allows you to charge a higher rent to pet owners. Automatically move that additional amount to a designated account. In this way, the amount of this cushion will correspond with how long the tenant stays and your potential expense. A per-animal rent increase might also discourage a tender-hearted resident from turning your building into a shelter for all the neighborhood strays.

This is why I can. Instead of giving yourself reasons why you can't do something, give yourself reasons why you can.

Day 87: Residential Property Taxes: Paying Only Your Fair Share

It's hard to argue that the collection of residential property taxes doesn't contribute to the quality of life in an area—but no one wants to pay more than his or her fair share. Take steps to see if your rate can be reduced. Attend hearings with your local tax-appeal board. Learn how and when your area's taxes are assessed and how you can lower them. Some local governments offer the convenience of dedicated staff to process property tax appeals and answer questions. The first step is usually to submit an appeal by mail or online, with lower tax rates for comparable properties attached. Next steps can vary widely from very simple to complex. Knowing where you are in the process can help you determine if you want to tackle it by yourself, or if it's worth hiring a professional. Don't get overcharged by default.

You deserve more. You deserve a better life—whether that means a better job, a healthier body, or more money. Work for it.

Day 88: Know Your Rental Market like the Back of Your Hand

Are the people living in your area buying more big-ticket items than last year or fewer? Are they saving more and spending less or vice versa? What's the average mortgage rate for this week? Is the unemployment rate for your immediate area higher or lower than it was six months ago? Maintaining an in-depth, intimate knowledge of the areas where your rental properties are located helps an owner to navigate current market conditions—as well as plan for the future. Updated knowledge of your market helps with everything from setting the most competitive rents to offering the best price for your next acquisition. Watching trends can help you to plan for raising or lowering rents—or purchasing more properties, if it seems like the market is heating up. An investor's luck comes from being prepared for opportunity.

It's never too late. No matter how old you are or how many opportunities you've passed up before, it's never too late to make a decision and get a fresh start.

Day 89: Maintaining Your Personal Investor Code of Ethics

Lawyers go through the qualifying process of being admitted to the bar to practice law. Unethical practices might result in being disbarred. Doctors recite the Hippocratic Oath as a vow to uphold ethical standards while engaging in their profession. Real estate agents seeking to acquire the designation of Realtor adhere to a certain code of ethics and standards of practice policy. Landlords are not bound by a set of uniform state or national professional standards. However, self-policing is in a property owner's best interests. Maintaining a high level of integrity is just as important in a successful real estate investor's career. The short-term benefits of cutting corners or trying to see what one can get away with are usually not worth the long-term damage to an investor's reputation.

There will always be challenges. No matter what you do in life, there will always be challenges—don't let one set get the better of you.

Day 90: It's Cheaper to Keep 'Em

Taking care of the customers a company already has might not seem as sexy or flashy as advertising campaigns to bring in new business. Savvy business owners, however, recognize the importance of customer retention, which is often undervalued. Recent studies have shown that at least 70 percent of companies say it's cheaper to retain a customer than to attract a new one. Landlords benefit by adopting some of the same kind of good customer-service practices used in corporate America. Not only should investors perform good customer service for current residents of their properties, they should display the same level of respect in relationships with business associates, clients, contractors, mortgage bankers, and any other parties involved in business transactions. Much of an investor's success in the field involves referrals. Giving people a reason to think of you first directly affects your bottom line.

> There's no "perfect" time. If you're waiting for the
> perfect moment, forget about it—there's no such thing.

Day 91: Ignorance of the Law Is No Excuse

In many areas of investment, such as stocks and bonds, there is no shortage of warnings and disclaimers about the possibility of financial losses. Ironically, the field of real estate investing is filled with infomercial gurus and other salespeople who want you to believe just the opposite. It is possible to make huge amounts of money in real estate, but smart investors understand that the process should never be oversimplified. Being a landlord involves certain risks, just like any other business enterprise. Familiarity with the laws and guidelines of your area helps to minimize those risks. Successful real estate investing involves more than just a contribution of capital. Investing in continuing your education regarding legal implications is just as important—if not more.

> There's no perfect plan. There are some definite flaws in your plan—but there are in every plan.

Day 92: Finding Your Niche

One of the *best* things about real estate investing is that it offers a wide array of choices from which a creative mind can choose. One of the *toughest* things about real estate investing is that it offers a wide array of choices from which a creative mind can choose. Oh, wait a minute—it looks like the biggest advantage can also be a disadvantage. This is only if you let it. You *can* create multiple streams of income through more than one area of real estate investing, but take care to get a handle on one before you start to expand your expertise. Deep, confident knowledge of one process usually produces more results than broad, shallow knowledge of many processes. Don't be a jack-of-all-trades and master of none.

Everybody starts somewhere. Nobody is born successful. Everyone starts somewhere and usually from the bottom.

Day 93: Counting Your Own Beans Might Not Be the Best Use of Your Time

Smart investors recognize the value of their own time. They know it can make more sense to delegate certain tasks, rather than for the investors to try to do them on their own. Preparing income taxes is right near the top of the list. Being familiar with how tax laws affect the operation of your business is extremely important. But spending too much time on staying updated on periodic changes to laws can interfere with your ability to make the *real money*. Find an expert tax professional with a gold-star reputation who specializes in working with real estate investors. Taxes are a big part of annual expenses. The money an experienced accountant can save you usually dwarfs the amount you pay for the professional's services.

*One step at a time. Don't try to do everything at once.
Reduce it to baby steps.*

Day 94: Don't Let Your Ego Block Your Success

You're smart. You're ambitious. You're resourceful. You've read all the books and attended all the workshops. You are more than ready to be a serious real estate investor. Or maybe you've already purchased one or more properties, and you're already in the game. Of course you can do it *all on your own*. But can you do it *well*? Investing in real estate can be fun, exciting, and profitable. It can also be complicated. Many who find that they are able to function completely as individuals notice that they don't reach the level of success they long for until they reach out to others. Connecting with a mentor or at least a supportive friend or family member who cares about your professional success is a sign of strength. It can help you through the rough patches along the way.

It can only get better. If it's hard at first, it can only get easier.

Day 95: Learning by Doing

There are many things prospective real estate investors can do to avoid potholes on the road to financial freedom. Read books, articles, blog posts, and other resources. Listen to webinars and audiobooks. Attend seminars and workshops. You should even talk to experienced investors to ask questions about what to expect. However, many aspects of investing depend on experiential learning. The thought of making mistakes can be scary, but it's a necessary part of mastering any worthwhile process. You should prepare as much as you can in advance, but there comes a point when you have to just jump in and take action. Real estate investing is not a spectator sport. It's a hands-on enterprise. Fight the temptation to fall into analysis paralysis. Explore your options. Decide which path seems right for you. Then get started. Ready, set, *go*!

Failure is temporary. If you fail, you're in good company—most successes come only after several rounds of failure.

Day 96: Finding a Contractor: No Need to Kiss Any Frogs

When searching for a contractor, phone books and random online searches are not your friends. The distant and impersonal nature of blind searching can make finding the right professional like finding a needle in a haystack. There are many more reliable ways to find a contractor you can trust to do the job that you need. Visit your local hardware store. Check out community message boards. Ask your friends, family, coworkers, and fellow church members. You can even check with the local housing authority or the real estate agent who sold you the property. Whether you hear it from a neighbor over the back fence or if it's dressed up in fancy new packaging like Yelp and Angie's List, word of mouth is still the best source of referrals by far. Go to sources *you* trust to find out the names *they* trust.

> Mistakes are learning opportunities. If you mess up, you can only become better for it.

Day 97: Narrowing Your Choices: Picking the Best-of-the-Best Contractor for Your Job

You've done your homework. You compiled a list of referrals from trusted sources and whittled it down to a few contractors in your area who specialize in the type of project you're planning. How do you choose the very best one for your job? The first step is the interview. The project has the potential to involve thousands of dollars and many years of enjoyment (or dissatisfaction). This process is as important as hiring an employee for a company. Make sure each contractor provides you with a detailed plan and a written estimate. Ask the contractor to show proof of insurance (if it is required in your area). Make sure you would feel comfortable with inviting this person into your home. Finally, avoid the contractor who offers the significantly lower bid or who appears to overpromise. What seems too good to be true often is.

Do just once what others say you can't do, and you will never pay attention to their limitations again.

Day 98: How Skilled Is That Prospective Contractor, *Really*?

Once you find a contractor you think you would like to work with, how can you gauge the quality of his or her work? After checking referrals, a common practice among savvy consumers is to find out if you can take a firsthand look at some of the contractor's other work. Here's a tip: try to view more than just a recently completed project. If possible, look at a range of work. Ask the contractor if you can view a site that is currently under construction. Also, ask to view an older project (at least five years old) to see if the contractor's work stands the test of time. Less reputable contractors might balk at this level of scrutiny. However, an experienced contractor who performs quality work is not likely to mind your due diligence.

> One of the most tragic things I know about human nature is that all of us tend to put off living. We are all dreaming of some magical rose garden over the horizon—instead of enjoying the roses blooming outside our windows today.

Day 99: Predictors for the Owner-Contractor Relationship

Remember that a great contractor is not just the one who is the most highly skilled. You also want someone who knows how to work with clients. Ask the contractor for a short list of current and previous clients. Contact those clients to ask about their working relationship with the contractor. Did they share good lines of communication? Were interactions pleasant? When and if problems arose, how were they handled? Was the job completed on budget and within the expected time frame? Did the contractor treat the owner with fairness and honesty? Even though contractors won't provide you with names of clients they had problems with, you can listen for subtle hints from the clients you are able to contact. The best time to gauge the "bedside manner" of a potential contractor is during the interview process—not once your project is under way.

Today is all you can control. Forget about what you did yesterday. Today is what matters.

Day 100: How Important Are Good Rent-Collection Practices?

Think of the flow of money through your rental property business. Of all the things that cost you money as an owner (mortgages, taxes, insurance, maintenance, repairs, licensing, trash pickup, utilities, property managers, etc.), rent revenue is just about the only puzzle piece that brings money in. All these other moving parts won't stop churning if your rents are not coming in consistently. Take a moment to reflect on what makes the importance of rent collection crystal clear. Arguing with and reminding late-paying tenants or tenants who don't pay is not enough if it doesn't result in real changes. Take a stark, rational look at what your rent-collection numbers mean for your long-term business goals. Take a deep breath and make the choice to take action to do what's needed to get the rents you deserve.

If it were easy, everyone would do it. Nothing worth doing is easy.

Day 101: Pardon Me, but That Halo Might Look a Little Crooked…

You were your church's most dedicated altar boy. Or you rose through the ranks of your Girl Scout troop and earned the most patches for integrity. You are such a Goody-Two-shoes that butter wouldn't melt in your mouth—but a prospective tenant doesn't know that. In light of rampant identity theft and fraud, we usually only view ourselves as potential victims. Do we ever stop to think that some might view us as potential suspects? Most renters dread the application process because they're required to provide their most private information to complete strangers—landlords like us. Alleviate their concerns by using a tenant-screening service such as SmartMove. This fast, secure service can vet prospective tenants without the need to share information such as Social Security numbers and bank account numbers with the owner. The tenant's credit score is also spared a ding.

Someday is today. If you're like most people, you use the word *someday* to describe your goals and desires. Make today that someday.

Day 102: "But *Seemed* Like Such a Nice Guy..."

"I don't need to pay for tenant background and credit checks," a landlord brags to his or her cousin at the family reunion. "I have a sixth sense. I can *read* people. I can spot a bad tenant from a mile away." Well, except for that time the well-dressed electrical engineer he or she rented to paid the first month's rent and never paid again before being evicted. Or the time when the kindergarten teacher with the well-behaved children turned out to be on probation for a physical assault on his or her previous landlord. Don't depend on your gut feeling when you entrust your rental property and the health of your cash flow to a complete stranger. Companies such as TransUnion make it so fast, easy, and inexpensive to run checks online that there's no reason to hesitate about taking this crucial step.

Negative thoughts can't stop you. Your negative thoughts are just thoughts—nothing more.

Day 103: Reasons People Choose to Invest

Why do people choose to invest in real estate? The answer is obvious, of course. It's because everyone wants to make a ton of money for the rest of their lives. Right? Wrong. People have as many *reasons* to invest as there are *ways* to invest. Some people even have reasons not directly related to money. An individual might decide to buy and manage rental properties to address a need for affordable housing in the community. Some people just love the mental challenge of the game. Goals could be short term, medium term, or lifelong—and your goals determine your strategies and timelines. Whether you're a prospective investor or if you've already made one or more purchases, clarifying the reason *why* you want to invest is one of the most important steps to ensure real success.

You've done harder things. Think back to a time when you succeeded against the odds.

Day 104: Short-Term Investment Goals

Some individuals have relatively short-term plans for investing. Generating cash flow to pay down debt or to pay off an existing mortgage can be accomplished in a matter of a few years. "Good debt" produces income. "Bad debt"—for example, medical bills, credit cards, and personal loans—primarily costs you money. Some investors acquire good debt (such as an investment property) as a means to pay off bad debt. Although investing for any length of time involves a certain level of risk, keep in mind that short-term investment goals can result in more exposure. Medium- and long-term investors have more time to ride out bad markets and recover from underperforming investments. Strategies requiring less commitment, such as crowdfunding or wholesaling, can also be good options for short-term goals.

Everything has to be earned. You can't get anything in this life unless you work hard for it.

Day 105: Medium-Term Investment Goals

A Chicago couple uses a medium-term investment strategy. They bought one rental property within the same month that each of their three children was born. They nicknamed each building after the new baby as they added it to their portfolio. This couple carefully calculated expenses and projected cash flow to ensure each property would produce enough for each child's college tuition. They set up separate bank accounts and credit-card expense accounts for the individual buildings. They said this makes it more real to them when they're managing each building, versus keeping everything in one big pot. If a tenant doesn't pay rent for one month, they understand that the consequences to their cash flow are not abstract. They are more deeply motivated to manage their rentals effectively. When each property reaches its goal, they have the flexibility to sell it if they chose.

Action is a better regret than inaction. Making the wrong decision is always preferable to regretting never having done anything at all.

Day 106: Find Your Why

If your investment plans don't have an expiration date, you are most likely a long-term or even lifetime investor. This designation has nothing to do with how long you hold on to a particular property. Regardless of plans to buy and sell specific acquisitions, long-term investors foresee some form of investing as a part of their overall lifestyle. Some investors seek to replace income from a job, allowing the flexibility to travel or spend more quality time with family and friends. Other people choose long-term investing for wealth-building opportunities. Not only do they desire to create a financially comfortable life for themselves and their families, but this option can also provide the ability to pass on resources to loved ones, organizations, and charities as a legacy.

You don't need anyone's permission. If people think you're crazy, so be it.

Day 107: Find Out How Much You Can Afford *before* You Fall in Love with "That Perfect Property"

You saw a gorgeous, well-maintained, brick three-unit building with an Open House sign while driving home from the dentist. A closer look shows it's just as impressive on the inside. It's in a great area near good schools and shopping. You have a feeling this would be the perfect investment for you—how exciting! Your frustrating attempts to acquire financing, however, prove the price is outside your range. Banks and mortgage companies are in the business of lending money—not owning property. They have turned careful calculations to determine what you can afford into a near science to avoid foreclosure situations. Smart investors view the purchasing process with the same type of businesslike emotional detachment. Find out what you can afford before you start shopping for an investment property. Don't set yourself up for disappointment by letting your enthusiasm take the reins.

You're in control of your own destiny. You can decide who you want to become.

Day 108: Determining the Right Mortgage Product for You

How's your credit history? What's your income? How much existing debt are you carrying? How much of a down payment do you plan to apply? Fixed-rate or adjustable-rate mortgage? How long do you plan to hold this mortgage? There are many questions involved in finding the right type of mortgage for you. Some of these questions will be answered by hard figures on paper. Some answers will be determined by your personality and your lifestyle. Given the complexity of the process, it makes sense to connect with the best professional to help you navigate it. Try to find a mortgage banker or broker who specializes in working with investors, not just homebuyers. Better still, try to find a mortgage specialist who actually owns investment property and personally understands the unique needs of a real estate entrepreneur.

> There is no pass or fail. Nobody is grading you. You can't objectively "fail" at life, unless you never try anything.

Day 109: How Do You Find the Best Area in Which to Invest?

After you clarify why you're investing and get preapproved for the amount of mortgage you can afford, the next step is to figure out where to buy. Some people try to keep it simple by investing very close to where they already live. These individuals might be limiting their potential return on investment by not researching the market. What if the neighborhood on the other side of town from where you live offers greater opportunities? You can only find out by doing your due diligence. Start by talking to a Realtor. The best choice is one who works with investors or actually owns property. Ask where he or she invests and where the Realtor's clients invest. If possible, ask if you can talk to those investors directly. Tap into real estate social networking sites, such as BiggerPockets.com. Networking is the key to selecting the best area.

> Boring decisions get boring results. Make an exciting decision.

Day 110: No, Not Location Again!

Once you determine how to get the highest use from the property itself, step back and take a look at the surrounding area. What's that phrase that has been beaten into the ground since it first appeared in a *Chicago Tribune* real estate ad in 1926? You've heard it a million times—but that's only because it's so true. The three most important things about real estate *really are* location, location, location!
Research the future value of a prospective purchase. Are there major nearby infrastructure improvements (mainly to transportation)? Does local political leadership encourage growth and stability? Does the area attract a financially stable demographic? What's the median income? Are there other factors to indicate this area is in demand for buyers and renters? Even the most gorgeous property in the world is boosted—or limited—in value depending on where it's found.

The risk is worth it. Know that risks are real, but the potential benefits are worth them.

Day 111: Still Looking for Your Type?

Many investors only give a passing thought to what property type they would like to specialize in. Property types include single-family homes, townhomes, condos, and multiple-family buildings (from two units to commercial complexes housing dozens of families). Some investors even doubt the need to specialize in a particular property type, choosing instead to buy whatever appears to be a "good deal." This strategy might work well for some. Investors who want to grow their business to a larger scale, however, often benefit from figuring out which single business model works best for them. Then the investors repeat that first success over and over until they have perfected it—before adding additional models. Narrowing down the type of property you would like to work with helps you to focus your search and maximize your efforts.

Discipline feels better than regret. Discipline is hard, but it's easier to deal with than regret.

Day 112: Who Is Your Soul Mate?

Different property types are affected by different factors, for example, the profile of the tenants they attract. Multiple-unit buildings are a more likely choice for individuals than single-family homes. Townhomes might draw young professionals seeking privacy who are not ready to make a big purchase. Single-family homes attract (you guessed it!) single families.

Before you buy your next property, it might help to first form a rough idea of what type of renter you prefer. Who will be your market? College students? Young families? Single professionals? Retirees? Individuals with special mobility needs? Remember that you will be working to perfect your marketing strategies at the same time that you're acquiring properties. Determining the ideal renter you are trying to attract will help you to laser focus your purchasing and marketing efforts.

Many good ideas seem crazy or impossible at first. Yours is no different.

Day 113: Use the 10 Percent Rule

Some investors have gotten the task of narrowing a list of potential properties down to a science. They apply a measurement called the 10 percent rule. First, determine the average monthly rent for the prospective property. Take into account amenities such as on-site gyms, designated parking, and other features, as well as the number of bedrooms and baths. You can get this type of information from online tools such as those offered by Zillow or Trulia, but finding an experienced real estate professional who specializes in working with investors is usually your best bet. Next, multiply the average monthly rent by twelve months to get the average annual rent income. Now divide that number into the asking price. You're looking for a number that is 0.10 (10 percent) or higher. Properties not indicating this minimum return can be crossed off your list in favor of more profitable opportunities.

You've got support—friends, family, colleagues—even if they think you're crazy. You can always find support in networking groups, support groups, and other community resources.

Day 114: Is This Your To-Do Visual?

Many of us daydream about things we want to accomplish, where we want to be in the future, and what type of lifestyle we desire. If these thoughts only float through our minds when we're stuck in traffic or as an escape from the boss's forty-five-minute PowerPoint on sales projections, will they ever come to fruition? The best way to jumpstart our habits into completing necessary tasks and achieving our goals is to put it all down on paper. In today's world, it is easy to pound them out on your laptop, tablet, or smartphone. How you put them down doesn't matter. There's just something about the connection between the eye and the brain that motivates us toward taking action. Making your daily to-do list and your long-term goals real—for your eyes to see—helps your brain to put the wheels in motion.

Experience is always valuable. Even if your mission doesn't turn out the way you'd expected, you'll walk away with experience.

Day 115: What Makes Us Rich?

Our achievements are not just about the number of zeros on our bank statements. Real success involves a healthy mind, body, and spirit. Prayer, meditation, or some kind of focused mental and physical concentration recharges our batteries and puts our challenges into perspective. Staying positive about what we welcome into our future is balanced with gratitude for the good that already surrounds us. Whether you have one dollar or one billion, what makes you rich right now? Regularly remind yourself of what makes you grateful in your life. Further still, reflect on the reasons why you're grateful for those things. Never stop developing yourself. Try listening to podcasts/audiobooks or reading as little as twenty pages a day to quickly increase your knowledge. Being positive, peaceful, passionate, and physically active is worth a king's ransom.

> Hard work is its own reward. You'll feel good just for
> making the attempt.

Day 116: What Really Builds Your Net Worth?

There is real truth to the old saying "Your network determines your net worth." Network and collaborate with other high achievers. Make it a habit to meet or connect with one new person every day within the field of real estate. Go to meetings, workshops, or presentations. You can even reach out to quality people on social media. Don't limit your outreach to other investors; also include those involved in other facets of real estate (attorneys, mortgage specialists, contractors, etc.). You never know what type of fresh perspective they can share. Human beings feed off the energy of the people around them—that's why we're often warned to choose our friends carefully when we're young. Make sure the circle of people you regularly connect with in your life includes a healthy percentage of people with similar vision.

Every day counts. Today, tomorrow, and the next day are all steps toward your end goal.

Day 117: Find Your Accountability Partner

Would you feel more motivated to reach your investing goals if you knew someone was checking your progress? Can you see yourself helping someone else move toward his or her own goals by serving in that role for someone else? Why not be intentional about creating this kind of mutually beneficial relationship? Some of the most successful and effective leaders do just that. Find a mentor or even another person at roughly your same level of achievement. Schedule a weekly catch-up session. Discuss each person's goals. Focus on progress or setbacks in the course of reaching goals. Set new goals as you reach the old ones, or be honest if you're still not where you want to be. The point of this consistent connection is for you to hold each other accountable by sharing your experiences with someone who cares about your success.

What you see matters more than what others see. Forget about what others think—prioritize what you think.

Day 118: The Lights Are on, but No One's Home: Insuring Vacant Properties

Investors generally do everything they can to avoid vacancies in their properties—almost by definition. There are some situations when vacancies are expected. If a property is undergoing renovation, the renter lives part of the year in another country, a rental is between tenants, or a vacation home is between seasons, owners realize that special care must be taken. However, it involves more than just physical precautions such as installing security systems to prevent break-ins or winterizing toilets and draining pipes in cold weather. Many are not aware that there are special insurance requirements for vacant buildings. Did you know that many standard insurance policies allow the insurance company to lower or even cancel coverage if a property is vacant for as little as a few weeks? Don't take chances. Ask your agent about coverage options with names like "Peril Protection" or "Vacancy Permission."

There is no problem that can't be overcome. Everything can be solved or worked around.

Day 119: "I Get by with a Little Help from My Friends"

When dedicated owners work hard to maintain their properties, the last thing they want to see is an influx of gangs and crime in the area. One problem building can lower the quality of life on a whole block. It's in every local government's best interests to provide services and support to help owners and residents curb crime before it gains a foothold. Some local police departments offer crime-abatement workshops for landlords. Some cities such as Chicago have entire government units dedicated to owner accountability. When necessary, they target irresponsible owners who turn a blind eye to crimes committed on and around their properties. City attorneys review police reports, meet with witnesses, and speak to neighborhood groups to determine the problem spots. Then they work to build cases against the offenders. Build relationships with local officials to head off problems before they start.

Ordinary actions make an ordinary life. Nobody wants to be ordinary. Don't let yourself be.

Day 120: And the Walls Came Tumbling

We've all seen them. Buildings with crumbling facades, cracks in the foundation, or leaning walls. The first thing we think is, "You know, someone should really tear that one down." Properties like these are not just an eyesore. They can pose a serious threat to the safety of the surrounding community. And they decrease your property value. Absentee owners don't seem to realize that the responsibility for the condition of a building does not end with losing the desire to maintain it. The municipal demolition unit often fines these owners. If the issue is not addressed, some cities can put the property in receivership to complete the repairs. When a property is beyond repair and the owner still refuses to cooperate, some local governments can demolish the building and redirect the cost to the owner by placing a lien on the property.

Everything can be improved. Even if you start out rough, you can always make improvements to your approach.

Day 121: Conservation Groups

Being a property owner requires a special type of committed, ambitious, resourceful person who is willing to put in work. It's a hard truth that not everyone is up to the task. Unfortunately, some don't acknowledge that reality until they're already in possession of a piece of property with no plans for a viable exit strategy. In addition, the death or disability of a competent owner can lead to years of legal battles between expectant heirs. Buildings might remain unkempt and fall into disrepair in the meantime. Housing abandonment and issues with the transfer of ownership can create problems for owners and residents of nearby properties. Local fire departments, police departments, and departments of health, human services, and housing and economic development often form conservation groups to proactively protect housing stock and promote the quality of life in affected areas.

You can learn whatever you need to know. Free resources are plentiful.

Day 122: Don't Run Afoul of Zoning Ordinances

Wait a minute—is your neighbor renting out his or her unheated, detached garage to a couple of college students? In Minnesota? In January? And is there a string of cars lined up and down your street waiting to be serviced at the Unauthorized Residential Car Repair Spot your other neighbor set up in his or her driveway? You haven't checked the rulebook lately, but you're fairly certain things like this are not allowed. Who's responsible for making the rules? Local zoning boards are charged with creating certain restrictions to let would-be entrepreneurs know what won't fly. Common offenses include illegally converting unapproved areas into living spaces and use of property for nonpermitted business activities. Authorities have the ability to seek injunctive relief, impose civil penalties, or even initiate prosecution for those who run afoul of zoning ordinances. Cutting corners is not worth it when the stakes are high.

You can master whatever you need to do. Practice can make you good at anything.

Day 123: If You Buy Only *One Book* on Real Estate Investing…You Would Be Making a Huge Mistake!

What's *the* best book out there on real estate investing? That's easy—it's the one you're reading now! But seriously, infomercial gurus and cable TV reality shows are on a constant mission to make it seem as if wannabe investors can go from zero experience to effortlessly managing properties. This can also be done in their sleep and only on weekends, while they kick back in their recliners with their feet up before the big game comes on. All they need to do is buy that book, sign up for that program, or join that website.

There is no "get-rich-quick" book that can take the place of careful study and hands-on experience. Each resource offers a different and valuable piece to the puzzle. Creating sustainable success in real estate requires deep, consistent, and ongoing education from a variety of sources. Real learning is a process, not a single act.

Willpower is all in your head. You can have all the willpower you want—you just have to want it.

Day 124: Advocate for Yourself

Two little letters: *no*. Who would think they could be so hard to say sometimes? Yet many of us struggle with setting boundaries for what others expect of us—whether we're saying it to the tenant who asks for a chance to pay late for the third time this year, the contractor who wants you to pay half up front and the other half when the job is complete, or the mortgage specialist who tries to steer you into a loan product that you know doesn't suit your needs. Be firm about protecting your interests. When we hesitate to say no, we allow others to set our schedules, lay out our plans, and spend our money—to their advantage, not our own.

You know what you want. Know what your end goals are, and visualize them.

Day 125: Don't Get Left Behind

"Oh sure, I'll get around to reading those books I bought about effective property management," you promise yourself. In the meantime, your reading list has grown long enough to wrap around your building and tie it in a nice bow. We're familiar with the pay-ourselves-first approach to saving and budgeting our money. The principle also applies to how we spend our time in building our investing careers through reading and self-development. Be intentional. Take a systematic approach. Treat it like a job. Set a schedule, show up on time, and work at it like you're vying for a promotion. Keep in mind that the other investor is creating time to stay on top of real estate trends and best practices. Don't get left behind when it comes to keeping your rental business competitive.

Feelings are the products of thoughts. If you're scared or unsure, know that these are feelings generated by your thoughts, and then you can control them.

Day 126: America's Most Popular Small Business

Many people who have never tried investing lined up to tell you it wasn't a good idea. You stepped over all the wrong information. You moved beyond other people's projections of their own fears disguised as friendly advice. Today is the day. You're on your way to sign the mortgage documents. You made a brave choice by taking a different route from skeptical coworkers and friends, but you never need to feel alone. You're stepping into great company. Some experts call being a landlord "America's most popular small business." When you get out there and start connecting with other owners, you'll find that it's true. Congratulate yourself for having the grit and determination to take the step millions of others only talk and dream about.

Trying and failing is better than doing nothing. This is universally true.

Day 127: Improve Your Surroundings by Sharing Your Roof

Choosing to invest in multifamily living can provide more than just cash flow. It can help a new investor in a very personal way by allowing the investor to qualify for a higher mortgage. This can make it possible to afford living in a more desirable area. Let's say a renter who is single and has only a modest income decides to buy a single-family house to live in. The bank would likely preapprove that renter for a modest mortgage because an individual with only one source of income poses a higher risk. However, if that renter chooses to go beyond the personal need for housing to purchase a multiple-unit property, the bank can count expected rents as additional income and increase the amount of the mortgage it's willing to offer. Improve your surroundings by sharing your roof.

> You are whoever you want to be. There's nothing stopping you from being who you want to be.

Day 128: Setting Your Sights

The great majority of people who buy single-family homes (SFHs) are simply owners who plan to occupy the property. Many of the remaining SFHs are purchased by smaller independent investors who choose not to make the leap to larger properties. These investors can get nervous about the price tag and the scale of large buildings, in addition to the amount of work it takes to maintain them. At the other end of the spectrum, professional investors and companies tend to set their sights much higher. They often prefer commercial investing, which includes buildings with five to one hundred units or more. What does that leave? Two- to four-unit properties are the lovely little diamonds that are sometimes overlooked. Smart, independent investors love the opportunity to add these money-making gems to their portfolios. Compared to SFHs, the cash often flows a little faster.

Your life is a product of your decisions. Make the ones that matter.

Day 129: The Broken Windows Theory

Cyclones of litter are formed by every breeze. Untamed shrubs have taken on a life of their own. Overflowing garbage cans are seductively beckoning to squirrels. The grass is tall enough to fatten cattle.
"I don't know why Chuck keeps hinting that I should trim these bushes," Jim ponders as he lounges in his hammock. "He must have control issues."
Frustration over the condition of a neighbor's property has been a source of conflict since time eternal, but it's not just about the cosmetic aspect. It's more than just eyesores or even sanitation hazards. Neglect sends a message to would-be vandals and criminals as strong and clear as Batman's bat signal streaking across a midnight sky. The "broken windows theory" argues that if thugs see one broken window, they'll be tempted to break more. Visible deterioration in neighborhoods indicates residents who will tolerate disorder.

You're better than you were yesterday. You're older, wiser, and more experienced than you've ever been before.

Day 130: Choosing the Right Flooring Is the Foundation of Any Good Rehab Project (Um, No Pun Intended)

Many new rehabbers struggle with where to draw the line between overinvesting and undervaluing. Several factors influence what type of flooring is best, including the value of the property (is it a luxury?), the intended purpose of the property (is it a high-traffic rental?), and the intended use of the specific room.

Believe it or not, even climate or geographical location can be major factors. Hardwood flooring and carpet are avoided in hot, humid areas. Carpeting is a popular temperature insulator in colder areas and a popular noise insulator on second floors from the sound of overhead traffic. However, the potential for stains and odors makes carpet a bad choice for rentals. Kitchen and bathroom flooring should be moisture and mold resistant. Make sure to install flooring that is in proportion to the value and the use of your investment.

Nothing great happens overnight. Work and patience are your friends.

Day 131: Adequate Apartment for Rent

"Step right up for the greatest, nicest apartment around. It has some bedrooms and a bathroom or two. We're offering the best special EVER! Call for details. DON'T MISS THIS REALLY GOOD UNIT! CALL WHEN YOU'RE READY!"
Weak advertisements, where everything that *can* go wrong *does* go wrong, won't get units rented. Don't be vague about features to attract more queries. It only wastes your time and the prospective tenant's time. Avoid generalities. Be specific about what makes your place special. Saying a place is "minutes from downtown" is much more engaging than noting that it has a "great location." If you offer appealing amenities, such as an in-unit laundry, a designated parking space, or free high-speed Internet, say so! Avoid all capital letters, as used in the example of a poor ad here, because it looks like a sign of desperation. Be honest and direct, but do your best to stand out from the crowd.

Once you get started, it will be easier. You'll feel more motivated once you get rolling.

Day 132: The Original Social Network—Weaving the Fabric of a Social Structure

Never mind Facebook and MySpace. The decisions of renters have been influenced by the *original* social networks since the first handshake between an owner and a tenant. Considering the effects on their relationships with loved ones is at the top of many tenants' priority lists. Renters also often remain in one location or seek a new location based on the best options for their children's education. Providing stability and not breaking the special bonds of friendships their young ones have formed are also important. Or a renter might choose to live in an apartment close to an aging parent to spend more quality time. Sometimes decisions are influenced across generations, such as when a renter chooses to live near a parent for help with caring for the renter's children. Proximity to extended family and friends rounds out the circle, causing people to put down roots.

Reward yourself when you're done. Even small rewards can be great motivators.

Day 133: A Match Made in Rental Heaven

You might not always be aware of the bad experiences tenants had with less professional landlords before they were lucky enough to find you. You could be that wonderful needle in a haystack to a satisfied tenant. It shows when you care about your property and are responsive to tenants' needs. Now that they've found you, why would they ever want to let you go? If tenants like one another as much as they like you, then you have yourself a winning combination. Renters breathe a sigh of relief when they can settle into a pleasant living environment. Your building is a rental community. And when all community members are on the same page—including you, the residents, and the property manager—it creates a welcoming atmosphere that people don't want to leave.

Maybe you're doing this for more than just yourself—
maybe it's for your family or community, for example.
Whatever *it* is, external motivation can be powerful.

Day 134: Love My Neighborhood, Love My Place

As a tenant strolls home from her office, she smiles at her good fortune. Her dentist is two blocks away. She found a hairstylist nearby who's able to put in her highlights just the way she likes them. She's surrounded by other people her age who have created an active and vibrant community of like-minded individuals. She can find great activities and jump right in when the mood strikes her. When she's feeling calm and peaceful, on the other hand, there are many places to foster quiet reflection. She can hardly believe that on top of all that, she lives in the loveliest apartment she's ever seen. It's a perfect size, and it's so well maintained that she feels as if it was built just for her. She opens the door to her very own space and knows she'll be there for a long time.

There are always more chances. If you screw up, you can always try again.

Day 135: Stability Leads to Longevity

Like people everywhere, renters are motivated by convenience. Whether gas prices are high or low, a short commute is the stuff of dreams. It's a great feeling when a tenant can roll over and hit the snooze button once or twice because the tenant lives in an apartment so close to his or her job. If that job is a stable one that pays well, then the tenant has it made. Moving can be a big hassle that many renters could do without. So why go through the process unless a major lifestyle change has made it a requirement? Tenants who have a stable lifestyle, including good employment and no big changes in romantic relationships, family size, or other life events, are much more likely to stay put in a rental unit.

If nothing else, this will make for a good story. You'll walk away with great memories and interesting anecdotes.

Day 136: The Risks and Rewards

Buying and investing in property does not come without risk. But nor does driving to work. Just as the accountants and actuaries can evaluate such stats as our geographic location, occupation, and gender and label us with a date of expiration, so can you evaluate your investment. From analysis of the property's potential to buy low/sell high, to the risk of your sketchy new tenant, you can add an analysis to each piece of the investment journey. You can develop a written strategy, a mission statement. Create a matrix for evaluating a property and reference weak areas. Create the alternate plan reference sheet when you learn how others mastered specific areas of concern. Keep up with current changes in government and market conditions to reduce the risks associated with low education. Stay thirsty for knowledge, my friend.

The power of positive thinking isn't just an adage—it's scientifically proven that positive thoughts (and the elimination of negative self-talk) can improve your mood, feelings, and performance. These thoughts should get you started doing whatever it is you need the motivation to do. The rest is up to you.

Day 137: Trello the Tech Hacker

For the visual learner and team, nothing beats adding a tool like Trello to your tool belt. Trello is a web-based application that uses a series of virtual whiteboards to organize your thoughts and the tasks at hand. You can use date-related boards for checklists that can easily be sorted and tracked to completion. Trello can be very beneficial to tactical learners setting up the visual plan. You can use it on a desktop, tablet, or smartphone. Snap a photo of something, and add it right into the boards you created. Consider using Trello as a prospect-management tool for new clients. Create boards for each new property, and once you develop a task list, you can easily rearrange the "reality" of the completion to the plan. Add cards to each of the boards to lay out your time and priorities, easily dragging and dropping these cards to aid in reevaluating your plan of attack. Create boards for each project, and include areas for plans such as screening new tenants and maintenance.

Love the life you have while you create the life of your dreams. Don't think you have to wait for the latter to start doing the former.

Day 138: Planning for the Project

Whether you do fix and flips or buy and hold, there is a time-sensitive series of steps that need to be managed. Becoming a pro at project management and the variety of software tools is an asset. Calculating how long the project should last and how much it will cost is an important part of the investment game. Know who is assigned to what task, and determine how long the estimated and actual duration is. Learning more about how to develop milestones, task lists, and tasks helps you organize projects into easily manageable days. Get more refined control with subtasks, recurring tasks, and dependencies. Develop a birds-eye view of the entire project, and allow related dependent tasks to be changed as emergencies occur. You can set up these types of plans in spreadsheets or visual project-management tools. Keeping records to track both the estimates and the actual time to completion helps you establish a historical reference to make better financial decisions as your experience grows.

Where you are is a result of who you were, but where you go depends entirely on who you choose to be.

Day 139: The Project-Management Cloud

Consider the many benefits of setting up your project in the software that keeps you best informed. The software will let you know what's been completed, as well as by whom, and what still needs to be done. Employees can provide updates as to what they're working on and share their updates with the project manager and team members. The software eliminates the need for status-update meetings and e-mails. ZoHo is a slick project-management tool that offers many benefits to the new user. Working in a drop-and-drag simple interface takes away some pains of understanding your first Gant Chart. When you use the online property-management features, the results of a delay by one contractor makes mastering the formula for delivering your projects on time and budget manageable. If you are investing for others, it gives you the perfect graphic interface to explain the triangle involved with cost, scope, and schedule.

Give up the need to be perfect for the opportunity to be authentic. Be who you are. Love who you are. Others will, too.

Day 140: How Do You Define "Real Estate Professional"?

What is a real estate professional? Someone on the street might say that anyone who sells real estate for a living is a real estate professional. If you ask the government, however, you'll get a very different, more complicated answer. The Internal Revenue Service defines a real estate professional as a person who spends at least seven hundred and fifty hours per year *and* more than 51 percent of his or her total working hours on real estate. This means you can't spend more time working at your day job than working at your rental business. You must also prove you "materially participate" in the management.

Why such a complicated definition? The Tax Reform Act of 1986 yanked away the label—and benefits—enjoyed by many self-proclaimed "real estate professionals." This is the government's attempt to eliminate tax shelters for those seeking to claim investment losses against active income from another occupation.

Replace your judgments with empathy, upgrade your complaining to gratitude, and trade in your fear for love.

Day 141: Fighting a Battle You Can Win!

Few phrases strike such panic into the hearts of real estate investors as *tax audit*. Deciding to file as a real estate professional while you have a full-time job is like taunting the Internal Revenue Service (IRS) with a red "audit me" flag. If you choose this route, you must be extremely well organized just in case you receive that audit-notification letter. The standard IRS requirement is that you must be hands on in the management of your rentals by spending at least five hundred hours operating *each* separate property. That's a tough standard for anyone to prove. Find yourself a good certified public accountant (CPA); your CPA can file an election to demonstrate that you're such an efficient superstar landlord that you were able to spend five hundred hours managing all your properties collectively. An upshot is that the election is valid until you revoke it.

> Be grateful for all that you have, accept all that you
> don't, and actively create all that you want.

Day 142: Floss Your Teeth, and Log Your Time

Keeping a detailed, accurate log of time spent managing your rental will be a godsend if you ever find yourself standing before a tax judge. This common CPA suggestion often causes involuntary eye-rolling by the average investor.
"Do I really need to do that?" we gripe.
We spend so much time maintaining our rentals that we feel as if we're married to them. Like an old ball and chain, our time is regularly spent in keeping everything running smoothly. It should be easy to just explain that to a tax auditor if the need ever arises, right? Guess again, my friend. Many years of discovering "creative" tax schemes have taught auditors to be skeptical. Convincing documentation is a must. Follow good advice. Just like a mother who reminds us to floss after every meal, your accountant can tell you, "You'll thank me when you're older."

Life isn't about wishing you were somewhere or someone that you're not. Life is about enjoying where you are, loving who you are, and consistently improving both.

Day 143: How Important Are Property Taxes to Cash Flow?

Less experienced investors tend to focus on the purchase price, expected rents, and rehab costs when it comes to analyzing cash flow for a property. Next to your mortgage, however, the taxes on your rental property are your biggest fixed expense. To say it's important to keep an eye on fluctuations and to look for ways to reduce those taxes would be the understatement of the year. Taxes alone can make the difference between a profitable investment and one that sucks your wallet dry. Before you make a purchase, commit to reviewing one to five deals each day for one month by hand or by using an online cash-flow calculator like one that can be found at BiggerPockets.com. Making it a habit to practice analyzing the cash flow on deals will make you an expert in your investing area in a very short time.

They say misery loves company, but so does mediocrity. Don't let the limiting beliefs of others limit what's possible for you.

Day 144: Investing Success Can Lead to Branching Out

Once you've mastered your local area, you might decide to branch out. Start by reviewing the property taxes in the new target area. Compare averages using annual reports like those offered by RealtyTrac. A recent study showed some general trends. Southern states tend to have lower taxes than northern states. Taxes usually decrease the further you move from urban centers. Beware of pockets of variations, however. Never assume property tax rates for neighboring towns will be similar, especially if they're in different states. There are many examples of one town with high property values and high taxes bordering another with high property values and *low* taxes. A lower tax rate can even help you to afford a higher purchase price. Doesn't the lovely gem of a town with low taxes sound like a great place to consider buying an investment property?

> Don't worry about trying to impress people. Just focus on how you can add value to their lives.

Day 145: Renting in a College Town 101

Serving the rental needs of a college community can be an excellent business model, but first examine the pros and cons. College towns offer nice amenities to young students experiencing their first taste of independence and the well-read professor seeking to satisfy an adventurous curiosity. This creates a large tenant pool. Available units in high demand keep rents stable and minimize vacancies. Areas are pedestrian friendly and have good transportation. The flip side is that students tend to change housing each year, resulting in high turnover rates. Above-normal wear and tear is the norm. Units are harder to rent in the off-season. Excessive alcohol use and immaturity often lead to noise complaints and other rule violations. As long as you have a clear understanding that the rental income you receive would be anything but "passive," this investment strategy could have a big payoff for you.

The moment you accept responsibility for everything in your life is the moment you tap into your power to change anything in your life.

Day 146: Working Title: Working with a Virtual Assistant

You went into business not just to achieve financial freedom. You wanted an outlet for your creative mind. Your vision has the potential to become legendary. One day the real estate gurus will seek out your advice—but first, you need to scan and file all these contractor receipts. Spending too much time bogged down with the minutiae of running your business leaves little time to learn and study and plan for growth. Working with a virtual assistant (VA) saves you the cost and commitment of taking on a full-time employee until you grow to a scale where you can afford to pay health insurance and other employee-related costs. You can pay on a project-by-project basis. Because VAs work from home, there's no need for expensive office space. Creativity is your strong suit (not pushing papers), so get some assistance.

Every single one of us already has everything we need to be the happiest we could ever be; it's simply up to us to remember that in every moment.

Day 147: Direct Mail: Making Sure Your Letter Is the One They Open

You climb down from the ladder for the sixth time in an hour to grab a notepad and promise never to start a direct-mail campaign in the middle of a rehab project again. It's exciting that your first round of letters has produced so many interested-seller calls, but painting ceilings and fielding inquiries from owners in preforeclosure just don't mix. Not responding quickly when those calls start coming in can cause lost leads and a waste of your time and effort. Timing and several other considerations can increase the success of your campaign. Commit to sending at least seven rounds (trim down your list if necessary). Determine your market. Craft an engaging message that speaks to that market. Honestly assess your budget and decide if it allows you to hire help. Direct mail can boost your business, but only when executed efficiently.

There is nothing to fear because you cannot fail. You can only learn, grow, and become better than you've ever been before.

Day 148: Supporting Our Service Members

Providing housing to military personnel can be a great way to use your business to assist the brave men and women of our country's armed forces. More service members are choosing to forego living on traditional bases to use special rent vouchers in the private market. Understanding special situations in advance can make life easier for both the applicant and you, the landlord. Semifrequent relocations might require the service person to submit a long-distance application. Use websites that allow for e-signatures. Some personnel might not have previous landlord references. Accept a letter signed by a commanding officer instead. This provides a reference and also confirms active military status. After reviewing the letter, follow up with a phone call to ask about the service member's work record and personality. Perform the standard credit and background checks. Show your patriotism. Rent to a hero.

Know that wherever you are in your life right now is both temporary and exactly where you're supposed to be.

Day 149: How Do You Eat an Elephant? One Mouthful at a Time…

When you start working toward any goal, fight the urge to do too much at once. The biggest key is to start small—not just small, but *tiny*. Begin with a task that is so easy that it's ridiculous. Can you read ten pages of a property-management book each day? Can you stick to logging on to one online investor webinar each week? Can you commit to attending one investor networking event each month? Achieving success is a matter of building productive habits. Building a habit starts with consistent, repetitive action. Repetitive action starts by taking on a small task. Taking on a task involves deciding to do something you can easily stick to and performing that tiny task over and over again. Tiny, consistent actions build such a strong foundation that you can't fail.

> Even when life is difficult or challenging—especially when life is difficult and challenging—the present is always an opportunity for us to learn, grow, and become better than we've ever been before.

Day 150: Focus! Focus! Focus!

You want to generate enough real estate income to leave your job within ten years. Great! You plan to start with a few wholesale deals, fix and flip a few properties, and then buy and hold a few more—within the next twelve months. Creative, ambitious people can get burned out when the passion for their goals takes them in too many directions at once. Studies find that the supposed high levels of productivity from multitasking are largely a myth. Trying to complete multiple projects at the same time drains your focus and energy—the two most important factors in successfully achieving your goals. You *can* reach a point in your investing career when you can manage more than one enterprise at a time, but reaching that level of expertise is a process. Don't try to tackle too much when you're starting out.

Who you're becoming is far more important than what you're doing. And yet, it is what you're doing that is determining who you're becoming.

Day 151: Ask Yourself *Why* You Want It

Why did you choose real estate investing? Do you want to provide for your loved ones? Are you looking to make charitable contributions to worthy organizations? Do you want to improve your community? Or are you just tired of struggling to make ends meet? If you're willing to make the sacrifice and put in the effort to reach your goals, you're entitled to determine your own dream. What charges your batteries? What makes you smile? What brings you joy? You might invest just to prove you can. Or maybe you want to spend one month a year relaxing on an island beach, drinking from a hollowed-out pineapple with a little pink umbrella. Even as you use your resources to benefit others, don't be afraid to say you expect your investing to provide a more comfortable life for *you*.

Make bold moves toward your dreams each day, refuse to stop, and nothing can stop you.

Day 152: How *Bad* Do You Want It?

It's not enough to go through the steps to learn your business and to make it grow. Only part of the process is technical. To keep your plans humming along, you have to plug them into a power source. Emotion feeds dreams. Sustaining yourself on your journey requires your excitement, enthusiasm, and unwavering desire to see your wishes come true. As you meet with obstacles to your goals, the only way to stick to the plan is to make sure that you want it deeply. Don't panic if your enthusiasm dips when you go through a rough patch or if it seems like things are not happening fast enough. Reenergize yourself by meditating on what got you excited in the first place. Then reclaim your zest and keep going. A driving passion fuels a dream much farther than a lukewarm hope.

Average people let their emotions dictate their actions, whereas achievers let their commitments dictate their actions.

Day 153: Tell the World

There's nothing like a public declaration to keep you on track. We can make and break a dozen promises to ourselves behind closed doors and never lose sleep. Sometimes peer pressure can lead to positive results. There's just something about the human need to save face in the eyes of our peers that raises our accountability to another level. It doesn't matter how you do it. Tell your family, friends, coworkers, fellow church members, or anyone who cares enough to see you succeed. Post in an online forum or start a blog. Schedule a regular e-mail blast. You can even propose a weekly column in your neighborhood newspaper. Regularly report your successes, but also don't be afraid to say when you fall short of your expectations. Encouraging words from unexpected sources can be just what you need to get back in the saddle.

If you have the belief that you can do it, you will surely acquire the capacity to do it, even if you may not have it at the beginning.

Day 154: What Makes Investing Fun

What are the regular tasks that make investing fun for you? Do you like window shopping for new properties online? Do you like interacting with tenants and providing services that exceed their expectations? Does researching a potential new investing area give you the same feeling you used to get when you opened a brand-new box of crayons? Or perhaps you're a number cruncher who likes to analyze the cash flow on a prospective property. Finding pleasure in small tasks every day is the key to making investing not just a way to make a living but a regular part of your lifestyle. Real estate investing can be as fun and exciting as it can be challenging. It's not really work if you're having fun. And if you're having fun, time flies by while you reach success after success.

It takes courage to grow up and become who you really are.

Day 155: Curb Your Enthusiasm to Get a Stronger Start

A great book or a fascinating conversation just helped you discover that real estate investing is right for you. Great decision! But don't start setting up your limited liability company (LLC) just yet. Give yourself a little time to prepare for your new career. You can even use this time to examine some bad habits that could slow your progress. Just like any big endeavor, the chances for success increase if you take the time to create a plan before you jump in with both feet. Set a specific date in the near future (up to a month) to get started. Mark it on your calendar to build anticipation and focus. Once you do start, harness your enthusiasm and set your dial for a slow release. A deliberate and sustainable start to your investing career is more likely to lead to long-term success than an impulsive and overcharged one.

Great minds have great purposes; others have wishes. Little minds are tamed and subdued by misfortune, but great minds rise above them.

Day 156: Post It Where You Can See It

When you open your eyes in the morning, it's there. When you stand in the mirror polishing those pearly whites, it's there. When you let down your car visor to keep the sun out of your eyes, it's there. It's your mantra, in big, bold letters—just a few words to remind you and keep you on track for what you're trying to do:

"Buy my first property."
"Buy my twentieth property."
"Close three to five deals per month."
"Reduce vacancies by 10 percent."
"Achieve a $5,000 monthly cash flow."
"Quit my day job."

Adding a specific date or deadline makes it more concrete. You can even kick it up a notch by saying your mantra aloud when your eyes come to rest on it. Your brain will be visually and audibly stimulated to maintain a subconscious level of excitement and anticipation.

I don't know the key to success, but the key to failure is trying to please everybody.

Day 157: Reading for Inspiration

There's a huge market for stories of people who have overcome challenges to achieve success. From world-famous public figures to people who live in our towns or neighborhoods, others who have succeeded nourish our eternal optimism. Even the most self-assured person benefits from hearing about another who has paved the way in his or her field. Reading not only that another person has held the same kinds of dreams you held but that the person was able to make them a reality sets you on a concrete foundation that what you desire is possible. Do an online search of real estate investor success stories. Use resources such as Zen Habits. Read books, articles, and blogs. The admiration and positive energy you send out for those who have already succeeded today will return to you in the not-too-distant future when an investor reads about your success.

If you don't make the time to work on creating the life you want, you're eventually going to be forced to spend a *lot* of time dealing with a life you *don't* want.

Day 158: Change Your Own Mind

The traditional path taught you to pursue an education only to get a good job. You've made the brave decision to pave your own road to financial freedom. The path that trained you to make your living as an employee came with very different messages from what you need to be an investor. One brave decision won't erase a lifetime of conditioning. Lingering thoughts might tell you it would be less trouble to work a nine-to-five job, or other types of negative thoughts might creep in. Prepare to recognize and address them. Be intentional about really analyzing the way you think. Retrain your brain. For a few days, keep a tally of each time you get discouraged with your investing or if you get an urge to quit. Stamp out the negative thought, and immediately replace it with an encouraging one.

The start is what stops most people.

Day 159: Keeping Yourself on Track

Being able to visually track your progress can be one of the most rewarding (or the most humbling) habits to keep you on the straight and narrow. Use a wall or desk calendar or create a simple spreadsheet that you can mark each day as you accomplish specific tasks. You'll subconsciously want to avoid too many days without an X. Take it one step further by adding minigoals to aim for to your spreadsheet. As you check off each day's progress, these baby steps lead up to minigoals, which lead to even bigger goals and successes. The value of this daily ritual is hard to overestimate. It's like giving yourself your own report card. If you're not satisfied with the marks you give yourself today, there's no need to get discouraged. You can always work harder to win your own favor tomorrow.

*Happiness is not something you postpone for the future;
it is something you design for the present.*

Day 160: Sustaining Your Motivation

Ever hear the phrase "creature of habit"? The human animal turns actions into habits through repetition. Even still, there will be days when you're tempted to break the good habits you worked so hard to develop. That's a natural human tendency, too. There might also be times when travel or emergencies or family obligations prevent you from completing a daily real estate investing task. Don't get too anxious that you'll lose your momentum if you miss a day or two here and there. No sweat. Just follow this simple rule: never skip three days in a row. Getting from where you are to where you want to be is a process that requires a long-lasting, slow-burning fire of motivation. Don't panic if the flame flickers. Just make sure to keep giving it more fuel the following day.

A difficult time can be more readily endured if we retain the conviction that our existence holds a purpose—a cause to pursue, a person to love, a goal to achieve.

Day 161: You Deserve a Reward

You laid out your plan. You took the necessary steps despite a few rough patches. Now here you stand with your first major success. Great job! What's next? Immediately put your head down and get back to work, you say? No way! Not just yet. You deserve a reward for the fruits of your labor. Don't just wait for the big events. Maintaining your momentum should involve minirewards for your minisuccesses along the way. Make sure your rewards are healthy and in proportion to what you have achieved. Don't overreward or underreward your efforts. Make sure your treats to yourself are sustainable and don't detract from your overall goals. Write down a reward schedule, which will motivate you even more, because then you will know what you have to look forward to. Your first reward could be just for getting started!

We all have dreams. But in order to make dreams come into reality, it takes an awful lot of determination, dedication, self-discipline, and effort.

Day 162: Get Help from an Expert

If you're lucky, you have friends and family who love and support you. They want to see you reach your goals, but sometimes you have to branch out to round out your support structure. Although affection and encouragement are wonderful, connecting with an expert in your field to provide technical expertise and knowledge can take your investing career to another level. Look for a reputable coach who can mentor you. Be very careful to find someone with a well-established track record. Or you can look for a class taught by a professional at a community college or online to teach you the fundamentals of building and managing your portfolio. If you're able to afford it, don't fret about the expense. Contributing to your long-term real estate career is an investment likely to pay for itself many times over once applied.

It is during our failures that we discover our true desire for success.

Day 163: How Do You Define Success?

What does success mean for *you*? Sounds like a strange question, but not everyone defines it the same way. How will you know when you achieve it if you don't know what *your success* looks like? We often spend too much time focusing on the tough parts of getting to where we want to be. Why not spend more time picturing where we actually want to be? Start developing your vision of the product of your dreams. Picture it down to the smallest details. Don't be afraid to take a page from the junior high school playbook. Consider creating a vision board with cut-and-paste images of what success looks like to you. Bring in all five of your senses. How does it look, sound, taste, feel, and smell? Making your target as real as possible draws it closer to you.

*So long as there is breath in me, that long I will persist.
For now, I know one of the greatest principles of success;
if I persist long enough, I will win.*

—Og Mandino

Day 164: Finding a Goal Partner

Sustaining self-motivation all on your own is not easy. Your enthusiasm might ebb and flow depending on what situations you're facing. Sometimes reaching for success can feel like a lonely prospect, but it doesn't have to be. People all around us are trying to reach goals as well. Throw in the Internet, and the community of strivers increases beyond measure. Find someone who is willing to be your goal partner, whether it's a friend, family member, or someone from your social media circle. Connect with a specific individual who can help you get through the low points, such as tenant disputes, repair issues, or evictions. It's even better when you find someone in your field with similar goals. In that case, you can share not only motivation, but also professional tips and resources to help each other along the way.

Show me a person who doesn't make mistakes, and I'll show you a person who doesn't do anything.

Day 165: Don't Wake the Sleeping Giant They Call the IRS

Popular culture paints tax audits as one of the life's greatest headaches. You do not want that kind of drama in your life. Besides, no one wants to overpay because they were not careful enough with keeping documentation. You can reduce the chances that you'll show up on Uncle Sam's radar if you follow a few simple rules. Pay special attention to tracking deductible expenses relating to managing your rentals. Although many local authorities apply property taxes in arrears, your federal income taxes should reflect the year when you actually paid them. If your mortgage lender escrows your taxes, you file for the taxes you actually paid. Be careful to claim the correct amount for your mortgage interest deduction. OK—maybe the rules are not actually "simple," but making the effort to understand them might just keep you out of trouble.

Too many people are thinking the grass is greener on the other side of the fence, when they ought to just water the grass they are standing on.

Day 166: Tax Tips for Nonaverage Years

Some long-term investors choose a slow and steady path to building a portfolio. They prefer a gradual accumulation of properties every few years. For this strategy, the tax implications in an average year can become fairly straightforward and routine. However, special attention must be paid in the years when buying, selling, or refinancing a property. In the case of refinancing, be sure to deduct points over the life of the new loan. When a property is sold, remember to pay capital-gains taxes on any profit. A new investor can use a first-time buyer tax credit to purchase an owner-occupied multiple-unit building, but keep in mind the repayment schedule in the following years. Learn the IRS guidelines on the tax credit if a property was sold or if you decide to stop using it as a primary residence within a certain time frame after purchasing.

Losers live in the past. Winners learn from the past and enjoy working in the present toward the future.

Day 167: Don't Listen to Kermit or Uncle Leo

Your Uncle Leo thought it was a crazy idea. Who on earth puts solar panels on their roof? What he doesn't know about are all the benefits to property owners of doing good things for the environment. The federal government encourages owners to improve efficiency by offering incentives. In addition to the long-term savings on energy bills, some improvements are eligible for tax credits up to 10 percent. The installation of certain items such as small wind-energy systems, solar water heaters, solar electric systems, energy-efficient heating and cooling systems, or geothermal systems can allow you to file for the Residential Energy Efficient Property Credit. Consult with your tax advisor on how to use Form 5695. Contrary to what Uncle Leo and Kermit the Frog try to tell you, it *is* easy being green.

Learn to appreciate what you have before time makes you appreciate what you had.

Day 168: Your Home Is Your Castle—and Your Office

Certain factors relating to the home-office tax deduction cause some investors to question if it's even worth it to apply. Guidelines can appear complicated to someone who is unfamiliar. Part of the deduction might need to be recaptured if the sale of your property produces a profit. This deduction appearing on your returns could draw the attention of IRS representatives. On top of all that, the benefits don't add up to a high dollar amount. Some investors, on the other hand, want to claim every dollar to which they are entitled. A new home-office deduction rule makes it easier to choose that option. Eligible investors can deduct five dollars per square foot up to three hundred feet of office space. The maximum is $1,500 per year. These simplified guidelines might justify taking the time to make the claim.

The content of your character is your choice. Day by day, what you choose, what you think, and what you do is who you become.

Day 169: Put Yourself First to Benefit Who and What's Important

The idea of putting yourself first can lead to uncomfortable associations. Compare it to taking a flight with a small child, though. Remember the first time you heard the flight attendant explain oxygen-mask procedures? Passengers are supposed to secure their own masks first before tending to children. Logically, the best way to effectively take care of those we care about is to first keep ourselves on firm footing. It's obvious to include family, friends, and loved ones in this category of those who matter to us. It also relates to business partners, clients, customers, tenants, and any other important relationships in your life. Further still, this applies to putting your best self forward to grow your business. Adequately maintaining our mental, physical, and spiritual health puts us in the best position to provide for life's priorities.

> I fear not the man who has practiced ten thousand kicks once, but I fear the man who has practiced one kick ten thousand times.

Day 170: What You Put in Is What You Get Out

You see it on TV. Late-night gurus try to convince viewers they can become highly profitable investors with "zero effort" and "zero investment." Online ads promise that anyone can become a wealthy real estate mogul overnight. Browse the titles of your local bookstore to learn how to be a "weekend landlord" or how to practice "landlording while you sleep." Any novice can wake up, buy a random property, sit back, and hope the money starts rolling in. Being a successful owner with a plan to build real wealth, however, is not a hobby. "Weekend effort" only produces "weekend profits." Or less!

Every investor with limited experience can be successful, but they must meet the learning curve head on to reach higher levels of expertise. Putting in the effort to learn the craft of investing is unavoidable—but the benefits can be beyond imagination.

Often the difference between a successful person and a failure is not that one has better abilities or ideas but the courage that one has to bet on one's ideas, to take a calculated risk—and to act.

Day 171: A Day's Worth of Effort Each Day

What can you do today to increase your success as an investor? Set aside thoughts of the properties you would like to buy and hold next year. Never mind the properties you would like to fix and flip in the next six months. What action can you take to get one step closer to your ultimate goal *today*? Attend a landlord training. Watch an online webinar. Read one chapter of a property-management book. When you're tackling these tasks, don't be discouraged if progress seems slow. Each phone call you make, each open house you attend, each potential property you analyze for cash flow increases your knowledge. Beautiful beaches are formed one grain of sand at a time. Each small step gets you closer to where you want to be.

A life spent making mistakes is not only more honorable but more useful than a life spent doing nothing.

—George Bernard Shaw

Day 172: Success Reflects Outward

Good habits and success are contagious. When you start to make progress, it shows. Your hard work inspires the efforts of others around you. Your circle sees you when you struggle to reach a goal. Your process is up close and personal to them. When you finally break through, those around you can feel the same sense of accomplishment that you do. This gives them a boost to make their own desires feel even more attainable. In turn, the positive energy they feel from their successes gets redirected back to you. The best way to raise morale in your social circle is to engage in mutual encouragement. Share your setbacks when a little moral support could help you to get back in gear. Share your successes to illustrate that dedication produces real results. It's a win-win situation when positive vibes are multiplied.

The starting point of all achievement is desire. Keep this constantly in mind. Weak desires bring weak results, just as a small fire makes a small amount of heat.

Day 173: The Investing Road Less Traveled

Traditional forms of real estate investing, such as residential rentals, have proven track records of producing profits when well executed. Some adventurous entrepreneurs enjoy getting off the beaten path. They know that opportunities might also lie in trends that are still becoming household ideas. The best time to profit is before the whole world gets involved. Migration *back* to the suburbs, tiny houses, green architecture, redevelopment of urban parking lots, replacement of aged public infrastructure, and urban agriculture are just some of the market-related trends that have been gaining popularity in recent years. The buzz around alternative-niche financial products, such as peer-to-peer lending, transactional lenders, hard-money lenders, and real estate crowdfunding, also continues to grow. Make sure to do your due diligence, though. Remember that some trends have as much of a chance to fizzle as they have to fly.

> Don't wait for something big to occur. Start where you are, with what you have, and that will always lead you into something greater.

Day 174: Accessing OPM

Savvy investors understand the power of leverage, or using other people's money (OPM). Whether you have experience but no capital, or you have funds you want to supplement, or you have cash but prefer the flexibility of financing with investor funds, you must bring your game to be trusted with OPM. But how do you get it? First, you need to gain an ear. Meet investors at networking functions. What's your elevator speech? Develop a strong opening where you clearly and briefly communicate the opportunity within the first thirty seconds. Once interest is piqued, build rapport by telling a relevant and engaging story. Review how they can benefit from the deal. Share your track record and past successes. Remember that you're not just selling the idea, but you're also marketing yourself and your ability to produce a good return on their investment.

> Ninety-nine percent of failures come from people who have the habit of making excuses.
>
> —George W. Carver

Day 175: Prepare Yourself before You Call Your Agent

Long gone are the days when the only way to know which properties were for sale was to drive past a lawn sign or get a printed copy of listings from a real estate agent. Today, all you need is a computer and Internet access to feel like a kid in a candy store. There are many sites that list available properties, as well as sold, rented, and expired listings. Each site also features other unique information to round out the investing picture of a potential property or area.

Although there's still a high value to adding a real estate professional to your investing team, you can become a better-educated investor by researching properties before you bring in your agent to initiate a transaction.

When the world says, "Give up," hope whispers, "Try it one more time."

Day 176: Stay Educated with Online Investor Resources

Even at times when you're not planning to make a purchase, staying abreast of your market helps you make better choices when it's time to buy. Realtor.com, the official site of the National Association of Realtors, provides assessed values of properties in an area. Craigslist is a great place to find "for sale by owner" properties. Auction.com features, of course, real estate up for auction, including notes, real estate owned (REO) properties, new construction, foreclosures, commercial/residential/luxury real estate, foreclosures, and raw land. LoopNet.com features commercial property. RealtyTrac.com is the go-to place for info on foreclosures. Propertyshark.com offers a wealth of information on property records and neighborhood information. Trulia.com provides crime stats, school stats, and info on market trends. Use online resources from the comfort of your home to become an expert on your target market.

There are no limits. There are plateaus, but you must not stay there; you must go beyond them. If it kills you, it kills you. A man or woman must constantly exceed his or her level.

Day 177: Find the Right Team

Hire people who fit into a team culture. Look for cooperation and a willingness to see the big-picture goals for your real estate investment strategies. Let everyone know where you're going—this means both employees and contractors are clear on the goals and buy into the plan. Establish clear expectations. Make sure everyone understands that it's the result of the team's work that counts. Add rewards and bonuses to your compensation based on the ability to achieve quarterly and annual goals. Provide recognition based on each contribution to these efforts. Encourage honest, frank discussions that solicit new ideas and suggestions to better achieve success. Keep morale high. Look for new partnerships and ventures that will stimulate a sense of purpose for your team. This allows the contractors and employees to see future opportunities for growth and adds to their prosperity. The right best hires do not cost a penny; they only contribute to your vision of success.

Inaction breeds doubt and fear. Action breeds confidence and courage. If you want to conquer fear, do not sit home and think about it. Go out and get busy.

Day 178: Maintain Your Momentum to Be Your Own Boss

This is what you dreamed of for so long. You carefully planned and prepared. You've done the hard work to build up your investing business, and you just made the decision that it's the right time to leave your nine-to-five job. You're ready to become a full-time real estate investor. Congratulations on creating an exit strategy, achieving your dreams, and getting out of the rat race! Before you know it, you'll be living a life of leisure and enjoying a lifestyle you hardly knew was possible. But not yet. Now is not the time to kick back and put your feet up. You're at an important growth stage. Don't lose your momentum. If you work as hard for yourself as you did for others today—for a just little while longer—the world will be yours tomorrow.

Nothing great has ever been achieved except by those who dared to believe that something inside them was superior to circumstances.

Day 179: With Financial Freedom Comes Responsibilities

You are the boss. There is no supervisor or crew chief or middle manager telling you when to come back from your lunch break, how many vacation days you can take this year, or how much money you can make. You make the rules.

That's the main reason most people decide to start a business in the first place—and managing rentals is America's top small business. How many people have dreamed of being in your shoes? This is a phenomenal achievement. Remember, though, that with freedom comes responsibility. As the saying goes, the difference between those who struggle and those who succeed is that successful people do what other people won't. When you work for yourself, you only answer to yourself. Make this your greatest strength, not your greatest weakness. Be accountable to *yourself* and your life plans.

Most people would rather be certain they're miserable than risk being happy.

Day 180: A Healthy Sense of Fear Motivates

Being an investor will involve downtime and a lot of time spent by yourself. How will you use your time when no one is looking over your shoulder? Surfing the web? Watching reality TV? The fact that no one is telling you what to do also means that no one is writing a check to you every two weeks. What do you fear most if your rental business is not as strong as you know it could be? A loss of revenue? Losing your ability to make your own decisions? How will it feel to go back to a nine-to-five job? A healthy sense of fear can be a powerful motivator. Use it to keep the fire burning under you and reconnect you with that sense of self-discipline.

The real person you are is revealed in the moments when you're certain no other person is watching. When no one is watching, you are driven by what you expect of yourself.

Day 181: When Success Comes, Don't Get Sidetracked

When you close that first big deal and you're holding that fat, beautiful check in your hands, you'll be excited and proud. You deserve this reward for your hard work and dedication. Savor the taste of triumph. Then go out and get that feeling again and again. Some investors decide to drift awhile after a big score. Remember that one check won't last forever. Keep adding fuel to keep the fire going. Set concrete, long-term goals to keep you on track. In this way, your minivictories along the way are less likely to make you hang up your work gloves and spend too much time celebrating. Use your victories to motivate you to keep working. Use the time to strengthen your professional connections with those involved in the successful deal and to plan for the next profitable project.

> Hold yourself responsible for a higher standard than anybody else expects of you. Never excuse yourself. Never pity yourself. Be a hard master to yourself—and be lenient to everybody else.

Day 182: A 1,000 Percent Return on Investment?

What rate of return on investment would make the average real estate investor do a little dance—10 percent, 15 percent, or 25 percent? What if there were an investment you could make that would give you a 1,000 percent return? It is possible—and it involves something even more valuable than money. This rate relates to the investment of your precious *time*. Studies have shown that every minute you spend creating a smart and effective plan saves you ten minutes of effort to make that plan a reality. If you put that in the context of money, this means that for every dollar you invested in a project, you would get ten dollars back. Some people say that time *is* money. Maximize your efforts by taking the time to develop a solid strategy before you get started.

Accept responsibility for your life. Know that it is you who will get you where you want to go—no one else.

Day 183: The Details in Your Plan

One approach to control your costs is to ensure the scope is well defined. The scope can be defined as the depth and detail of your view of the project. The key to ensuring costs are maintained is to ensure scope is defined to a sufficient level of detail and is written and reviewed in each project. Work with contractors who have enough history and experience to estimate a timeline range based on your building and the potential impact of changing weather conditions. You may mitigate risk by including penalty clauses for late delivery or incentives for early delivery. In a corporate project, stakeholders have expectations for deadlines; the same should be applied to your own personal project. Consider taking the time to conduct customer-reference calls and site visits to confirm that the potential vendor does a quality job with high customer satisfaction. The same process can be applied by contacting the city building authority and requesting customer testimonials and feedback. Reach out across your own social network and get feedback from others to ensure your expectations will be met.

> When life knocks you down, try to land on your back.
> Because if you can look up, you can get up.
>
> —Les Brown

Day 184: Transformation Takes Time

Why is it that sometimes lottery winners find themselves broke within a couple of years after their big payday, sometimes with even more debt than before they started? Why is it that sometimes people lose a lot of weight with a crash diet and then gain it all back and then some? The best way to make a new habit or lifestyle change stick for good is to embrace the careful and steady progress toward the goal. Trying to do an end run around the journey prevents you from growing into the type of person who can sustain these changes over a lifetime. Jim Rohn, the "father" of the motivational speaker movement, said, "It's not the money that makes the millionaire successful; it's what he or she had to become [as a person] to earn a million dollars."

You can't just sit and wait for people to give you that golden dream. You've got to get out there and make it happen for yourself.

Day 185: Implementing New Technology

Identify issues that will save your staff time and ultimately add to your efficiency. The investigation should highlight problems and identify new technology solutions in the marketplace. Go to your staff for their input; this will help them see that changes need to take place. Research the software options available and which solutions will work best with your business workflow and process. Back up all your data before you begin, and have a backup transitional plan for the actual conversion day. Do your best to minimize disruption. Ideally, you can incorporate training within some of the implementation tasks. Employees who set up their own systems are better able to keep them running and operate them. They may identify unexpected problems and find solutions. A final step for the successful introduction of new technology into an organization is to perform an evaluation of its performance once installed. There may be actual problems with the way the technology works, or there may be perceived problems for some users. An evaluation identifies both types of problems.

Make sure that your actions and behaviors live up to and reflect the words and ideas, promises, and commitments that come out of your mouth.

Day 186: The Strength of the Wolf Is the Pack

Partnerships are not for everyone; they require a lot of effort. You'll want to develop a list of qualities that contribute to partnership success. Research and investigate before the partnership to eliminate doubts and suspicion once you move forward. Learn to respect your partner's point of view. In every relationship there are differences, arguments, and complaints. Learn to not make an issue of the small stuff. Choose the hills on which you want to die. Learn to smile at everything else. A lot can happen in a single day, and both parties need to be aware of what is occurring with the other partner. Discussing daily events and future goals keeps the relationship growing and validates the reason you teamed up to begin with. The partnership should be well planned, and the arrangement should include all possibilities covered in the initial agreement itself. The agreement should include details such as roles and responsibilities, capital contributions, and profit splits. Also, it should include details about what should happen when the partnership ends. Partnership is not meant for everyone. Decide if you are a lone wolf or prefer the pack.

History has demonstrated that the most notable winners usually encountered heartbreaking obstacles before they triumphed. They won because they refused to become discouraged by their defeats.

Day 187: The Change Order

As noted by Wikipedia, "In project management, a change order is a component of the change management process whereby changes in the Scope of Work agreed to by the Owner, Contractor, and Architect/Engineer are implemented."

Common reasons for change orders will vary during your experience with real estate investment projects, but they will seldom disappear. It is best business practice to accept that change will impact your numbers and to do your best to buffer in a plan for it. When you get started, some projects will be incorrectly estimated. There will be forces and obstacles that require you to deviate from the original plan. You may have selected a contractor who is incapable of completing the required work within budget based on the timeline. There will be times when additional features or options are desired and requested. And of course, you may not have considered weather conditions that may contribute to delays. Detailing your project and carefully reviewing the impact of change on each milestone will help reduce the overall project-cost overruns and timeline.

> Don't be so quick to claim your limitations when you've never truly tested them.
>
> —Kevin Ngo

Day 188: Be a Great People Person

So much of being a successful investor involves great people skills. Keep a positive attitude. It not only keeps you in the right frame of mind, but positivity is contagious. Respect people and their time. Make use of the amazing power of *please* and *thank you*. Be sincere. Practice active listening. We have two ears and one mouth so that we can listen more than we speak. Make people feel special and that you value them. Even when you're having a tough day, try not to take out a bad mood on others. Whether you're a landlord maintaining good relationships with the residents of your building or a wholesaler working to gain the trust of distressed homeowners, how you interact with people directly impacts the level of success of your business.

> Keep away from people who try to belittle your ambitions. Small people always do that, but the really great make you feel that you, too, can become great.

Day 189: Do What You Love, and the Money Will Come

As the old saying goes, "Choose a career you love, and you'll never have to work another day in your life." Real estate can be more than just a way to make a buck. There are so many different strategies under the umbrella of real estate investing that all potential investors can find some route that gets them charged up. If you've been stuck in a rut for so long that you can't remember what you're passionate about, do an online search for good self-assessment tests. When you find the right investing vehicle, it can seem like everything just clicks. When you're doing something you love, you can't help but put your heart and soul into it. Make every moment count. Live a life that allows you to express the fullness of your best self, and the money will come.

> The attitude you have as a parent is what your kids will learn from more than what you tell them. They don't remember what you try to teach them. They remember what you are.

Day 190: Do Good Work to Reflect Yourself

Dr. Martin Luther King Jr. once said that even if your job is just a street sweeper, aim to be the best street sweeper you can be. People of good character try to master whatever vocation or field they choose, even down to the lowliest of duties. The same is true for investing. Not every task is glamorous, but each necessary task should be treated with importance. This doesn't mean that every job must be performed by your own hand. Even when you delegate responsibilities, it still takes careful attention to detail to make sure they are executed well. How you handle the details is a reflection of who you are. Bring meaning into what you do. Even when you're very good, always strive to get better.

> It isn't what you have or who you are or where you are or what you are doing that makes you happy or unhappy. It is what you think about.

Day 191: Have Integrity

Building a good name for yourself is a cornerstone of a long and productive investing career. A good reputation can open some doors for you that even money can't pry open. Always be mindful of how your words and actions represent you. Don't make promises carelessly. And when you make a promise, keep it. Everyone makes mistakes. If it happens, accept responsibility and own it. People appreciate it when others hold themselves accountable. Tell the truth even when it's tough. Make sure the choices you make consistently reflect your values. Try to be transparent and explain why things should be done a certain way. Never give people a valid reason to question your integrity. It takes time and effort to build a good reputation, but one can be destroyed in an instant.

Every great dream begins with a dreamer. Always remember that you have within you the strength, the patience, and the passion for reaching for the stars and for changing the world.

Day 192: Frustration and Negative Emotions

As a successful investor, you have to have your head in the game. But you also have to recognize how much of the game is in your head. You will experience a range of emotions, some resulting from stress. Understanding how you react to difficult situations can help you to manage those feelings. No matter how much you study and prepare in advance, you will encounter some failures along the way. Everyone does. The measure of your longevity will be how fast you bounce back and how much you learn from each situation. There will be things about the process that scare you. Examine those fears so that you can protect yourself from risk, but don't feed those fears and allow them to paralyze you. Making peace with the fact that not every day will be lollipops and sunshine puts tough times into perspective.

All who have accomplished great things have had a great aim and have fixed their gaze on a goal that was high, one that sometimes seemed impossible.

Day 193: Get Help and Give Help

The idea of the self-made person is a myth. No man or woman ever became successful without some type of help from someone, somewhere along the way. Asking for help is not a sign of weakness. It takes a strong person to acknowledge that he or she, like every other human, has limitations. Also, think of the flip side of the coin. Try to be ready and willing when someone seeks your assistance. Even as you're learning your craft and making your way down the path to becoming an expert investor, you might already serve as a role model for someone who hasn't gotten started. Being available to share your time and experience might help this person avoid some of the mistakes you made along the way. A wise investor recognizes the time to ask for help as well as the time to turn around and help others.

Each day is a new life. Seize it. Live it.

Day 194: Start by Connecting with *Local* Investors

National online investor communities are great, but be careful about where you get your information. Some online investors report only what works in their area without specifying where they're located. Real estate law is very local, and if you try to apply what works in one area to another area, you can find yourself on the wrong side of the law. For example, one investor "expert" blogger recently gave his readers the general advice not to rent to lawyers. He warned that lawyer tenants had a tendency to sue their landlords. What he didn't clarify is that he's based in Washington State, where this practice might be allowed. Local ordinances in some cities, such as Chicago, prevent landlords from discriminating against tenants based on their source of income. A Chicago owner who followed this "guru's" advice without further investigation could land in hot water. Network locally *first*.

To accomplish great things, we must not only act, but also dream, and not only plan, but also believe.

Day 195: Your Risk in Proportion to Your Experience

A new investor doesn't need to buy a twelve-unit building. No need to get ahead of yourself because you think you should play the role of the big-time mogul. Let your capital investment catch up with your experience instead of leading with your cash and letting your knowledge trail behind. Lower your risk. Start with a two-unit building. Live in one unit and rent the other to get the hang of it. If you're still renting or living with family, it's perfectly fine to make your first investment a single-family home for yourself. Spend six months or even a year or two getting accustomed to paying a mortgage. Learn the physical and financial aspects of managing a property. Turn that first home into a rental as you acquire more properties. It's fine to start small—just as long as you *start*.

If you're born poor, it's not your mistake. But if you die poor, it's your mistake.

Day 196: Break—or Prevent—Bad Habits to Decrease Stress

Income-tax preparation ranks at the top of many property owners' lists of dreaded tasks. Some owners throw all their receipts in a shoebox all year. Then they put off organizing their expenses and income until the April 15 deadline looms large and imposing, like a horror-movie villain. Let's be honest. This is not the best business practice. Not only does it cause unnecessary stress at tax time, but it also prevents you from tracking the status of your rental property throughout the year in case you need to make adjustments. If you already own property and you've been stuck on an annual cycle of struggling to file your taxes, don't let another year go by. If you're new to investing, don't wait until your portfolio includes ten buildings. Meet with an accountant and a lawyer to implement a good, manageable bookkeeping system.

Life is what we make it—always has been, always will be.

Day 197: Make Friends with Real Estate Jargon

Section 1031 exchange. Cash-on-cash return. Amortization. Cap rate. PITI. Comp. FSBO. If you're a new investor, enough unfamiliar terms might fly at you to make your head spin. Sometimes you might wonder if people are speaking another language. It's true. They *are*—and you should try to learn it as fast as you can! Some investing books list a glossary of terms. You could also try doing an online search of common real estate investing lingo. Not knowing the lingo can be like overhearing a conversation in another language while the speakers are *talking about you*! Just because you don't understand what's being said doesn't make it any less important to you personally. The more pieces of the puzzle you gather, the faster and the bigger will be the investing picture that comes into focus for you.

The best way to predict your future is to create it.

—Abraham Lincoln

Day 198: Real Estate Math Is Simple

Studies show that a common characteristic among the American public is the idea of "math anxiety." Corporations take great pains to stimulate interest in math-related disciplines among students. This aversion to math and calculations and percentages can steer some people away from investing because they don't trust their ability to crunch the numbers. Don't worry. You don't need a college degree to understand real estate math. Most of the calculations can be done by a fifth grader. There are tons of investment property calculators to be found online. You can just plug in the numbers, and the calculations are done for you. Even better, print out an online worksheet and analyze a couple of deals by hand. This old-fashioned method gets you up close and personal with the numbers to really understand how they work. Don't let math anxiety stand in the way of your financial freedom.

> Few people take objectives really seriously. They put average effort into too many things rather than superior thought and effort into a few important things. People who achieve the most are selective as well as determined.

Day 199: Sacrifice Today, Big Payoff Tomorrow

You might not like it, but it's better to hear it. The road to financial freedom is not paved with gold, so to speak. Or the journey toward real wealth won't always be milk and honey. Or, to make it plain, working your way to the lifestyle you want requires sacrifice, hard work, and long-term dedication. No matter what the late-night gurus say, the name of the game is deferred gratification. You might have to temporarily give up some of life's little luxuries, like a new car every couple of years or vacations abroad. It might involve grabbing a hammer and putting some sweat equity into your property. Many who have tried to use real estate as a get-rich scheme have learned the hard way that real success usually comes only with sustained effort over time.

You must take personal responsibility. You cannot change the circumstances, the seasons, or the wind, but you can change yourself.

Day 200: Keep Learning—Whichever Way You Choose

You hear it all the time. If you want to become successful in just about any field, you have to read, read, read. For any number of reasons, maybe you've never been a big fan of sitting in one place holding a book. Or maybe you simply believe you're unable to carve a significant block of time out of an overloaded schedule. In either case, try audiobooks. You can listen while you complete other tasks. Or listen to YouTube clips on investing. Instead of read, read, read, the real message is that you must learn, learn, learn. Whichever process you use, find ways to constantly expose yourself to new, updated information. You will be amazed—and very pleased—by how much your investor knowledge expands in just a short amount of time.

You never know how strong you are until being strong is the only choice you have.

Day 201: Do You *Have* to Hate Your Job to Love Investing?

Sometimes it might seem like all investors are looking for ways to quit their jobs and become full-time entrepreneurs, but this is not the case. Not all investors hate their bosses and long for a way to get out of the rat race *immediately*. Some do work that fulfills them, and they look forward to going into the office each day. Whereas some choose to invest as a career, others prefer to use it only as a vehicle to reach certain financial goals. Some forms of real estate investing are more time intensive than others, such as being a successful wholesaler. Some forms require moderate amounts of time, such as being a landlord. Other forms of investing, such as crowdfunding through real estate, require little time at all once the initial investment is made. Figure out how the different strategies might mesh with your other career goals.

Either take the chance and make achieving your dreams a possibility or don't, and make living with regret a certainty.

Day 202: Is It Really a Deal?

Having an app available to help you examine the best deal is a must as you are growing a portfolio. Moving quickly to make offers on good properties will be crucial. In the many changing peaks and valleys of the real estate investment cycle, knowing your sweet spot is key. Property Fixer is just one such tool. Apps make it helpful when driving around to scout properties, allowing you to do property analysis on-site. Don't make an offer without knowing the benefits. From free spreadsheets to free property analysis tools, look for reviews and verify performance meets your standards. These tools can offer calculations of sophisticated indicators, interactive reports, and even enable sharing on your social networks.

The happiness of your life depends upon the quality of your thoughts.

Day 203: A Fresh Alternative to Tracking Money

Track expenses, time, and setup billing in one spot. FreshBooks is a powerful new time saver the busy investor should check out. Use it to track projects, track billing, and assign expenses. Import and capture your bank and credit card expenses easily. Set up alerts for late payments. FreshBooks offers top-rate invoice-to-payment features. They ensure that invoices have been properly delivered to clients through e-mail tracking. Expenses are as quick as a snap. Simply click a picture of the receipt and attach the snap to an item in FreshBooks to log the expense. Implement time tracking for your maintenance team. You'll really like the handy estimate tool for interacting during rehab projects with your team. You can create an expense report to track monthly costs and monitor your balance sheet in real time. Invoices are simple to read and create. Reports can be exported to a CSV file and other popular formats for sharing with a tax adviser or accountant. Your customers get a really nice interface for viewing all their invoices online.

Life's challenges are not supposed to paralyze you; they're supposed to help you discover who you are.

Day 204: Break Habits and Visualize Success

The best way to lose the bad habit is to identify and own the negative habit. Taking ownership and acknowledging the issue begins your new path. Start a habit-breaking journal and write things down. Tracking the days and times of your habit can become a real awareness builder. Complete a written accounting of the positives and negatives of your habit. Include the impact on yourself, your friends, and family. Include the short- and long-term impacts of the habit. Begin to slowly establish a bait-and-switch plan. Find the item that can replace the habit and slowly introduce it into your day. Once you introduce the new healthy habit, slowly implement rewards. Keep it simple, and keep it small. Replacing bad habits can have measurable impacts on your stress. Visualize yourself crushing the habit, smiling, and enjoying your success.

Things work out best for those who make the best of how things work out.

Day 205: Your First Property

If you are a millennial, then saving is the last thing on your mind—especially if you are young. Youth, energy, and money seem eternal. But that's not true, and this is the time when you should save and invest for the future, because it is cheaper and will give you higher returns over time.
Age is on your side. Instead of wasting your money on partying while you are living in a dump, cut costs at this point of time in life because you can afford to do so. This time is ideal, when you are single and living costs are low. You can get houses for cheap. Do not misunderstand—real estate prices are on the rise. But there are plenty of distressed homes available for less than market value. Buy these, ensuring they are within your budget, and then make a killing as prices keep rising. If you intend to rent out your purchased property, you are setting yourself up nicely for a second source of income. Use this money to reinvest in your property, or use it to pay off other bills and debts.

It is not what they take away from you that counts. It's what you do with what you have left.

Day 206: Form the Line Here

Are you coming back to the office to empty your pockets to find important papers? Canvas can bring forms that were once a stack of paper and make them interactive. Convert your most needed paper maintenance forms and processes into a Canvas app and change the way you work. This tool will allow you to create the form and set it up in an instant. Take a look at the large list of templates available. They offer service orders, estimate sheets, carpet cleaning, building inspections, and waiver and release forms. With an image-capture feature and an e-signature, you'll quickly be building your own custom mobile app. Your daily operation will be forever impacted with efficiencies. While it is quite addictive to convert your team's process, keep in mind it can be pricier than other free options with the per-user cost.

You may never know what results come from your action. But if you do nothing, there will be no result.

Day 207: Paint the Picture of Your Perfect Rental

Start up a free account on Canvas and begin using real estate graphics without having technical design skills. You will only be limited by your own creativity. Canvas is an online platform that has taken the experts' tool and broken it down to its simplest form. With drag-and-drop features and a multitude of free graphics and flyers to choose from, you will add an amazing edge to your blog or social media posts. Consider sending a new prospect a custom-created presentation of your vacancy. Create an online listing sheet and add a matching open-house invite. The interface is easy enough to use on your tablet, and the results are amazing.

Remember you will not always win. Some days, the most resourceful individual will taste defeat. But there is, in this case, always tomorrow—after you have done your best to achieve success today.

Day 208: Drive Up to the Cloud

Cloud based. Free storage space. Accessible offline. What more could you want? Google Drive provides free access to documents, sheets, slides, forms, and drawing. But accessibility to those features pales in comparison to the collaborative ability that sets Google apart. The ability to allow multiple people to collaborate in real time from different locations is what makes Google Drive priceless for your business. So yes, there are competitors for Cloud-based storage space, but not many offer the quick convenience of multiple users. Share your welcome booklet and update your inspections for your resident reviews. "The greatest mistake you can make in life is to be continually fearing you will make one."

I've got a theory that if you give 100 percent all the time, somehow things will work out in the end.

Day 209: More Than Meets the Eye

At first it may seem that Google Docs is the same as any other document. While this is true to an extent, the ability to "share" the document with other people makes it key to any business. The real-time share feature allows anyone to view or edit the document at the same time that the owner of the document is making edits. The chat feature allows people to discuss changes as they are being made. There's no longer a need to switch between e-mailing and the document that you're working on. I'm sure you can find a better use for your time. A Google Doc can help when you do not have your computer close by.

Let us not be content to wait and see what will happen, but give us the determination to make the right things happen.

Day 210: Creativity and Action Build Wealth

The old expression "It takes money to make money" doesn't always apply. What is true is that it takes *creativity* to make money. The average person might view a problem as a roadblock. The most successful investors are the ones who encounter a problem and immediately try to develop ways to get around it. This is also a major difference in perspective that separates the rich and the poor. A person who starts out with no resources but builds wealth through creative choices is more likely to see long-term success than the person who is born with wealth but displays no creativity. Shift your thinking away from what *can't* be done, and focus more on seeking out ways that it *can* be done.

Never give up on what you really want to do. The person with big dreams is more powerful than the one with all the facts.

Day 211: Respect Investing as the Business It Is

Many landlords get into the business with the idea that it'll be a cakewalk. When they come up against the reality that investing is actually a business, some grow to resent the role. Owning and managing rental property can be relatively straightforward, but only if you establish your business on a firm foundation. Set up your systems and strive for efficiency. Once you gain expertise and develop your formal infrastructure to handle your investment properties, the time will come when they won't require as much close supervision. However, novice investors can't afford to view it as a hobby or pastime when they're starting out. It also can't be treated as a job with the privilege of clocking in and clocking out. Business is an enterprise that can bring you great rewards, but only if you take it seriously.

If you limit your choices only to what seems possible or reasonable, you disconnect yourself from what you truly want, and all that is left is a compromise.

Day 212: Successful Investors Are Committed Investors

The steps to finding success in investing are clear and simple. Of course, you should do your homework. Find out about the different investing strategies that exist. Pin down the best strategy that fits your goals and your lifestyle. The next step is just as important, if not *more* important, than the others. You have to *commit*. Ironically, many new investors overlook this step. This leads to results that fall short of their expectations. At this point, some disappointed investors will blame the strategy when the reality is that they didn't stick with it for long enough, or they didn't seriously apply what they learned. You might plan to become an investor for life, or you might want to invest for a few years to reach a certain financial goal. Either way, you must remain committed during the time period you choose to be an investor.

It is under the greatest adversity that there exists the greatest potential for doing good, both for oneself and others.

Day 213: No Need to Learn about Every Path to Investing before You Get Started

Some investors hesitate to get started in real estate because they feel they need to learn everything first. This is not the case. Compare investing to other fields. Even after years of formal education, a corporate lawyer is not likely to know all the ins and outs of environmental law, and a defense attorney might not know any more about estate-planning law than the average person on the street. Do a little investigating into the different paths to investing. Learn just enough to figure out which route is best for you and then focus on learning all you can about that one area. Next, take action on what you've learned. You can always add additional strategies to your plan once you become proficient at the first one. Those who are really good at something are the ones who find their niche and specialize in it.

> Perfect is not attainable, but it we chase perfection, we can catch excellence.
>
> —Vince Lombardi

Day 214: Old-Fashioned Ways to Sell

Being an investor is not just about acquisitions or purchasing property. Successful investors need to be just as knowledgeable about the selling side of real estate. It's a given that those who fix and flip and those who wholesale need to be intimately acquainted with best practices for seller transactions. Keep in mind, though, that even buy-and-hold investors who seek to build a portfolio with long-term purchases will need to engage in the selling process at one time or another. If you're looking to keep it simple, the old-school ways still work. You can list your property with a real estate agent or place an ad in the local classifieds section. Your neighborhood's free weekly might bring even more results than the citywide paper. Don't forget one of the simplest, oldest methods—the unassuming but highly effective yard sign.

Our greatest fear should not be of failure but of succeeding at things in life that don't really matter.

—Francis Chan

Day 215: Free Online Seller Resources

Many sellers are familiar with the fancy bells and whistles showcasing properties listed with professional real estate agents. Fewer realize they can create their own professional-looking websites for *free*. Increase the appeal by adding as many photos as possible (interior and exterior). Record a brief virtual tour to help a prospective buyer get a better sense of the proportions of space. List your properties individually on sites like Zillow, Trulia, Enormo, HotPads, Local.com, or Backpage. Or save yourself a huge amount of time by listing on Postlets, which will link to these other sites for you. Don't forget other free sites, such as eBay Classifieds, YouTube, ListedBy, and Craigslist. You can also create a "squeeze page," or a landing page, to gather contact information for potential buyers. In this case, you'll have a ready, go-to list of possible buyers for marketing future properties on a regular basis.

> Why you? Because there's no one better. Why now? Because tomorrow isn't soon enough.
>
> DONNA BRAZILE

Day 216: Paid Online Resources for Selling

Despite the long list of free sites you can access to sell a property, don't underestimate the value of using a paid site. A relatively small fee charged to sellers to list a property on a reputable site might be well worth it if it increases the chances that a particular property will be sold. Well-established paid sites are working to earn the fees they charge to sellers. Because of this, some of these sites invest more in actively marketing themselves as a resource, which could ultimately draw more eyeballs to your listing. Try auction sites such as eBay Auction or Bid4Assets. You can also place ads on sites such as Google AdWords, BiggerPockets Marketplace, vFlyer, ForSaleByOwner.com, LandWatch, or other related sites.

> You have within you, right now, everything you need to deal with whatever the world can throw at you.
>
> —Brian Tracy

Day 217: Networking to Sell Your Property

A great way to sell your property in the short run and also build long-term connections is to put yourself in the company of people who love to buy real estate—or people who work with those who do. You would be surprised how easy they are to find. Visit your local property-management companies, real estate attorney offices, title companies, mortgage brokers, and even hard-money lenders. Join local real estate investor networks. Talking to other sellers in your area might even lead to results. If you meet a seller who is trying to sell a different type of property in a different section from yours, the potential for competition is removed, and a spirit of information sharing might develop. National online investor forums, such as that at BiggerPockets.com, might even help you to find local groups near you.

> A happy person is not a person in a certain set of circumstances, but rather a person with a certain set of attitudes.
>
> —Hugh Downs

Day 218: Off-the-Beaten-Path Ways to Sell Your Property

Just as there are many creative ways to find a property as a buyer, there are many nontraditional ways a seller can market a for-sale property. Some turn their vehicles into rolling billboards, advertising with strategically placed window stickers or magnetic signs as they go about their day. Some post business cards or flyers at local places where people congregate, such as restaurants, educational or religious institutions, or social organizations. Investors who specialize in buying the type of property you're offering might be found with a quick Google search. Some sellers even tout the benefits of their "diamond in the midst" directly to the surrounding neighbors by placing flyers in mailboxes. The tried-and-true method of seller financing might also open the door to many hopeful buyers who would love to make arrangements to buy your property.

> There is no such thing as a good idea unless it is developed and utilized.
>
> —Kekich Credo

Day 219: The Importance of Your Daily Routine

Routine. Habit. These words imply something done out of drudgery—an activity that you need to drag yourself through, something that needs to be done out of compulsion. But this is an idea that is horribly far from the truth. People who have not mastered the idea of a routine and worked consistently to master it are the ones who make statements such as these.

The advantage of a routine is that it helps you prioritize important things so that you do them first. It also reduces procrastination and decision fatigue. What is *decision fatigue*? Your mind can make a certain set of decisions per day. At work, you are constantly making one decision or another, and you often exhaust the quota of decisions that you can handle.

Routines help negate this habit. Routines take the act of doing something out of the realm of decision making and into the realm of something that always gets done at a certain time. The result is that you are able to do those activities that really matter and help you achieve more. You will find yourself wasting less time and using your time more fruitfully.

> Once a routine is set and you stick to it, you will slowly see the benefits.
> Destiny is not a thing to be waited for, but a thing to be achieved.
>
> —William Jennings Bryan

Day 220: Get Positive

To be able to make the most of every opportunity given to you and to take what comes your way, it is vital to have the right attitude. If you have the right attitude, then you will not see any obstacles, only paths and stepping-stones to success. So how does one cultivate this habit? Well, the mind is a very gullible thing, and if you consciously train it to look at certain events through a certain perspective, then it will do so and interpret events in that light. You may have seen examples of optical illusions in the past. Those are a perfect example of how gullible your mind can be. So the place to start is to build a positive attitude. How do you do that? You do so by saying something positive and good and visualizing it. It can be something as simple as, "Today is going to be the best day ever!" Statements like this set the tone for the day or at least put you in the right mind-set. Now, is whatever you say really going to happen? Of course not. But what it does is put you in a mind-set to always look at the brighter side, even if something goes wrong, and look for the silver lining in the clouds.

> Things may come to those who wait, but only the things left by those who hustle.
>
> —Abraham Lincoln

Day 221: Be Proactive

It is important to be positive and decide to take hold of the events in your life and not just react to them. Always start your day by focusing on *you* and what you need to do, what your state of mind is, and how to get things accomplished in the day. This way, you take ownership of the day and decide how you respond, and not vice versa. So don't take this habit lightly. Focus on things that help you perform better during the day and help you improve your skill sets. If you think that a time of meditation can help you organize your day, then start off doing that. Or if you want to invest in "sharpening your axe," then spend that time reading up on your skill set.

A simple way to avoid being reactive is to not check your e-mail the first thing in the morning or start working immediately on a project. If you do that, then you have to respond to any e-mails or project situations, and you will end up changing your schedule—making it entirely reactive, not proactive. So take your chance—grab the moment, and make it yours.

> The most creative act you will ever undertake is the act of creating yourself.
>
> —Deepak Chopra

Day 222: Mentally Prepare

Prepare yourself mentally for success. Think of positive instances that are happening and that will happen as a result of your actions. Visualize success and successful events in your life.
This will create a positive vibe and a positive attitude in everything you do. There are many people who are scared of success or who don't know how to respond to it or other favorable conditions. They end up behaving like a deer in the headlights, which can actually prevent them from utilizing successful circumstances. *You don't want to do that.* You want to grab opportunities when they come and be ready for success. In order to be successful, act as if you are already successful.

The height of your accomplishments is determined by the depth of your convictions.

Day 223: Face the Fear

Why is it important to face your fears? All of us have fears that prevent us from achieving the ultimate. Ask yourself, "What is my ultimate fear? What things am I most scared about? What is really the worst thing that could happen if [insert potential future bad situation here] were to come true?" And then imagine this event actually occurring. Once you face up to your fears, only then will you be able to overcome them. By thinking through potential situations and their outcomes, you'll likely see that most fears don't involve a life-or-death deal. It's a bit like being a dog catcher, overcoming a fear of dogs, and then using it to your advantage. Once you have mentally conquered your fear, nothing can hold you back. You can face anything that comes your way. That is one of the stepping-stones to success. So it is important to prepare mentally. If you fail to prepare, then you prepare to fail.

Perseverance is the hard work you do after you get tired of doing the hard work you already did.

—Newt Gingrich

Day 224: Read

There was a time when intelligent people were supposed to have massive libraries and impressive studies. Almost every major thinker of the eighteenth and nineteenth centuries would have been painted in their impressive studies. All of a sudden, the intellectual of our era has become the person who gets the maximum likes on his or her Facebook page or Twitter. Our generation has become fascinated by the Kardashians and Biebers of this age, a generation with stunted brains and easily distracted minds. It is important that we snap out of this reactive, intellectually stunting habit. One way to do this is to start reading. Just about anything will work for a start.

Read a page of your favorite novel or the editorial of a newsmagazine or something that is informative or gets you thinking—anything that gets you into a habit. Don't aim big—*just a page will do*. Read and then reflect on what you have read.

The plus points of reading are that it keeps you informed, stimulates your imaginative juices, and helps boost your intelligence and concentration. It helps you experience various events through the perspectives of other people.

The best way out is always through.

—Robert Frost

Day 225: Make Yourself Accountable

We have all had the experience of wanting to start some new habit or achieve something significant, approaching it with enthusiasm and then slacking off. How can you ensure that you'll stick to it? One way is through accountability. Make yourself accountable to someone, or get a mentor, someone you are comfortable with and who understands you. Or find three people you are comfortable with and who know you well. Talk to them, tell them what you intend to achieve and how they can help you, and verify that they understand you. Mentors understand your weaknesses and strengths. Thus, they can tell you where to put in some effort and where you may need to go easy on yourself. When you start doubting yourself or start slacking off, they can be really useful. So who can be your mentors? Who can hold you accountable? Establish mentor relationships and see your life transformed.

Obsessed is a word the lazy use to describe the dedicated.

Day 226: Write Today

Why is writing important? And what should you write about? Don't aim big. You don't have to be a Tolstoy right off the blocks. Start small. Just think back over the day and reflect on it. What was a good moment? What was the worst moment of the day? Could you have reacted differently to someone or some event? Could you have said something different? What did you achieve over the day? Is it all that you had planned for, or did you want something extra? One good way to start off is to try describing your day in a sentence. That will help you prioritize and analyze your day succinctly. Then you can keep expanding on that. Try to be regular in writing and set aside a part of the day for that activity specifically. In the beginning, you need to take time off to do this, or you will keep postponing it and never do it. Writing improves your creativity as well, and it helps improve your communication skills. It also helps improve your vocabulary. So if you want to achieve more in life, then it's time to start writing.

I do it because I can; I can because I want to; I want to because you said I couldn't.

Day 227: Set Up Your Categories

Categorize your plans. From purchases to property management, an investor accumulates many tasks, activities, and plans. A good way to approach planning is by making categories of activities: personal, professional, recreational, social, emotional, and spiritual. Then decide what you want to do in each of these spheres, and set up your ideas accordingly. Whatever your approach, you should have activities decided beforehand with a slot ascribed to each.

Even if you can't set aside full days to deal with certain issues, you can probably block off certain hours of the day to handle them (going back to breaking your day into chunks). This can give you the time you need to make headway in those particular areas—without putting your brain on overload.

A journey of a thousand miles begins with a single step.

Day 228: You Deserve a Break

Your mental image of a hardworking overachiever might be one of somebody hunched over a table or computer, slogging away for hours on end.
The human brain can work at peak performance levels for a maximum of twenty minutes. Beyond that, its efficiency decreases. So it makes sense to take a break every twenty to twenty-five minutes. Once you get back to your activity after a break, you have to recheck where you left off. This involves the brain recollecting what it was doing prior to the break. This strengthens the neural circuits and the mental associations, thus helping you to better remember the elements of your task. Another advantage is that it lets you take stock of the task and how you have done so far. It can help you increase efficiency and maintain focus.
Taking a break can add to your productivity.
Now, get set to watch your efficiency soar.

The future belongs to those who believe in the beauty of their dreams.

Day 229: Plan Your Week

The planning period starts from the beginning of the week. You can set aside either a Saturday or Sunday for this task (the end of the previous week or beginning of the new one). First, do a "mind dump"—put whatever you want to get done down on paper. Include all those things you want to do but never have time for. After that, include your daily activities, such as work, walking the dog, doing the dishes, and so forth. Then include once-a-week activities, such as going to a game, hosting a Sunday barbecue, and so forth. Next, separate all activities into those that are important and those that are not. Then start fitting them into various time slots throughout the week. Try to make sure that the important and priority tasks, such as a major project or a doctor's appointment, are slotted in first. Then put the other activities from your mind dump in the slots around these activities. Ensure that a time slot is provided for each activity. There should be no activity without a time slot. This may sound boring and stifling, but it will ensure that you are able to do what you plan to do, and contrary to popular belief, it will actually be liberating.

A healthy mind in a healthy body.

Day 230: Deep Breathing

Your mind needs a proper house to stay in, which is your body. Thus, it is vital to ensure that your body is at its optimum as well.
Practice deep breathing. The lungs act as a detoxifier by removing volatile toxins. Deep breathing also provides oxygen to the tissues and improves heart function, reducing stress-related effects. Deep breathing is a stress buster that you should practice daily. Learn to take a good deep breath. That's easy, you might say. But most of us do not breathe through the diaphragm, causing improper oxygenation and increasing the mechanical load on the breathing muscles.
To find your diaphragm, sit comfortably or lie on your back on the floor. Place your left hand on your upper chest and your right hand on your abdomen, in the "gap" of your rib cage. When you breathe in and out, your left hand should remain still, and only your right hand should move up and down. If your left hand is moving, your breathing is too shallow, and you are not using your diaphragm as you should. Try to alter your breathing, so that only your right hand moves as you breathe.
Last, but not the least, is to learn this art through practice. A good trick recommended by Tony Robbins is the one-four-two rule done three times a day for ten days: inhale for four seconds, hold for sixteen seconds, and then exhale for eight seconds. Keep breathing, friends.

In the end, what we regret most are the chances we never took.

Day 231: Eat Productive Foods

You are what you eat. Some foods require more of your body's resources for digestion, so avoiding these foods will help to keep you focused and alert. The brain functions best when a certain amount of glucose is present in the blood. If glucose levels are low, you will feel fatigued and tired. High glucose levels cause you to feel irritable and can lead to the release of insulin, which lowers glucose levels, again causing you to feel fatigued. The best foods are therefore those that maintain a steady glucose level of twenty-five grams, like a slow burn (in scientific parlance, they are called low-glycemic-index foods). Foods that will leave you feeling optimized include whole grains, nuts, avocados, tomatoes, raw carrots, and nearly everyone's favorite, dark chocolate. Start munching on these and watch yourself feel healthier, lighter, and more invigorated.

You were not born a winner, and you were not born a loser. You are what you make yourself to be.

Day 232: Drink More Water

Sixty percent of your body is composed of water. It's found in nearly every organ and in every fluid of your body. It's involved in almost all parts of body function, from digestion to circulation to removal of toxins from the body. It is the essence of life. This should be enough to make you carry a bottle of water. The benefits of water can be found everywhere. It is great for losing weight—ask any dieter. A glass of water before food cuts your appetite and thus your food intake. It helps your muscles grow and eliminates fatigue by washing out toxins. It is also good for the skin.

Here are a few tips for increasing your water intake:

- Carry a bottle with you at all times.
- Drink water with every meal.
- Eat more fruits and vegetables—cucumbers and watermelons, for example, have a high percentage of water, helping to keep you hydrated.

The Mayo Clinic recommends up to nine cups a day for women and thirteen cups a day for men. So chuck the coffee cups and head over to the cooler!

> Things don't go wrong and break your heart so you can become bitter and give up. They happen to break you down and build you up, so you can be all that you were intended to be.

Day 233: Have Some Tea

Real tea is derived from a plant called *Camellia sinensis* and comes in four varieties: green, black, white, and oolong. Anything else isn't tea—technically. What makes tea beneficial is the antioxidants it contains, called polyphenols. These are good for your heart. Antioxidants also help to prevent colorectal, stomach, small intestine, skin, lung, esophagus, pancreas, liver, ovarian, prostate, and oral cancers. Pheeew! Now that's a huge benefit. They improve exercise endurance because they help in utilization of fats during exercise. So if you are planning to run a marathon, then a cup of tea may be a good idea.

> People who say it cannot be done should not interrupt those who are doing it.

Day 234: Get Out of Your Chair

Research has proven that fidgety people live longer and healthier lives. It does not matter how much time you spend in the gym because the body gets accustomed to exercise after a certain point in time. But people who are always on the move or refuse to remain sedentary reap the maximum benefits. Why is this so? First, it is important to understand why sitting is so harmful. It has been found that sitting has an antigravity effect on the body that lowers its heart rate and muscle activity. This, in turn, leads to increased levels of cholesterols and triglycerides in the body because they are not metabolized, which can harm your heart. Six hours of continuous sitting daily can reduce your life span by seven years. Remember to stand once every hour. Move around and read that file. Use the stairs. Get outside for a break. Park your car farthest from the office and walk the distance.

You should aim to get about thirty minutes of activity per day. Now, what if you don't have thirty minutes to spare every day? You can break the activity into ten-minute intervals. These ten-minute intervals can even be done in the office. Health websites and magazines are replete with office workouts. You can check them out or do simple stretches to make sure you are on the move.

> Courage doesn't always roar. Sometimes courage is the quiet voice at the end of the day saying, "I will try again tomorrow."

Day 235: Exercise and Move

If I told you there was a healthy, cheap activity that you could do for just twenty minutes a day that would give you the benefit of a longer life and help prevent diabetes, heart disease, cancer, and brain disease, what would you say?

"Bring it on, buddy."

Yes, but that is in theory. In reality, what you'd likely say is, "I'm too tired, I have no time for it, or I'm too old for it. It's not for me."

The activity I'm talking about is *exercise*. Many would rather pay thousands of dollars for toxic drugs than do this pleasurable, enjoyable, stress-busting activity for just twenty minutes a day—which can be free. There are plenty of workouts on the Internet for busy people—for example, the ten-minute workout by Beach Body or the seven-minute workout. Multiple apps are available that can help you track your activity. You don't need expensive weights and gyms. All you need is your body and the will to do it. Just start. Exercising has never been as easy as it is now in the Internet era. And never has it been so vital. The trick is to stick it out for the first couple of weeks. Once you get hooked onto the endorphin high, you'll be looking forward to the exercise time. It might be tough to tear you away from the treadmill after that—two weeks is all it takes to get hooked. So get up and start doing something.

Strength doesn't come from what you can do. It comes from overcoming the things you once thought you couldn't.

Day 236: Find Time to Sleep

Sleep is extremely important to your overall health for a multitude of reasons. In the short term, not sleeping enough can affect your judgment, mood, and even your ability to retain information. In the long term, chronic sleep deprivation can lead to obesity, diabetes, cardiovascular disease, and even early death. To get a good night's sleep, you can limit your caffeine to early in the day and choose foods to eat late in the day that bring on sleep, such as bananas, oatmeal, and potatoes.

Two simple aspects of healthy sleep are getting enough and getting it during the same time frame each day (as much as possible). Remember that sleep is the most important activity today that can affect your day tomorrow.

If you argue for your limitations, sure enough, they're yours.

Day 237: Your Spiritual Well-Being

In the digital age, a proliferation of strategies and products claim to help in physical and mental well-being. But the one aspect that has really taken a beating in this fracas is spiritual well-being. It is an often ignored aspect in this physical age, where there is a hunger for the seen, and noise is cooler than silence. How does one look after one's spirit and ensure that one's moral bearings are not lost in this noise? *Get quiet. Try meditation.*

Meditation is necessary to get in touch with one's spirit. It's ideal if done daily. The best way is to keep quiet for twenty minutes or so and focus on one thing. It could be a positive or inspiring thought or even one's breathing. In the beginning, the mind will wander. But that is the whole point—to put mind over matter. As you keep pulling back the focus to the task at hand, your mind will slowly start to focus better, and you will be able to keep your physical and emotional impulses under control. Meditation thus has powerful effects on one's willpower. It also reduces stress, anxiety, and depression, according to Harvard University studies—even more reasons to give it a try if you haven't before. There are many guided meditations available for free online, and many people find that this is a great way to get started (or to enhance your practice).

YouTube is full of guided meditations. Once you start practicing meditation, you will become a more stable, calm person with a positive vibe that will rub off on those around you.

Action may not always bring happiness, but there is no happiness without action.

Day 238: Find a Well of Inspiration

Inspiration and motivation can come from many places—books, music, podcasts, videos, e-mails, or other people. All you have to do is find the one or ones that resonate most with you and commit to engaging with them—daily. Research has shown that inspiration can be activated, captured, and manipulated…and that it has a major effect on important life outcomes. Another way to get inspired involves repeating positive affirmations. So find a word or phrase that is empowering and motivating to you and repeat it over and over again to yourself.

> Every time you stay out late, every time you sleep in, every time you miss a workout, every time you don't give 100 percent, you make it that much easier for me to beat you.

Day 239: Practice Gratitude

We live in the age of "go get it." Being an ambitious go-getter is considered cool. It is common to be always on the hunt for the next big thing and to feel a sort of dissatisfaction with what you have. However, this attitude—although perhaps positive in the short term—is not a healthy one and can damage your spiritual well-being. There are so many things that we should be thankful for. If you woke up tomorrow and only had the things you were thankful for today, what would you have?

By spending time each day expressing gratitude for all the blessings in your life, you do two things. First, you recognize that even though things may not be exactly as you'd like, you are fortunate to have what you do. This leads to optimism and a positive attitude, no matter what the situation. Second, the more blessings you are thankful for, the more you draw in or attract. It's as if they multiply. Come up with a list of all the things that you are grateful for and go over it when you get up in the morning and again before you go to bed at night. You can also take it one step further and pick someone from your past you're grateful for, get in touch with that person, and let him or her know how you feel. Imagine the impact this could have on the other person…and you!

> One of the most common causes of failure is the habit of quitting when one is overtaken by temporary defeat.

Day 240: Wiki How

As normal human beings, we possess a couple of skills that we have learned over a lifetime. And most of us are pretty happy with this limited skill set. However, we are living in an age of knowledge explosion, and there are a lot of benefits of training yourself to learn something new daily. Learning something new makes you happier in the long term. Although it may cause you a little stress in the short term, the end result is a higher level of life satisfaction, making it more than worth the initial uneasiness. It also widens our perspectives and gives us a wider skill set to adapt to new situations. It makes us innovative and inspiring, confident, and interesting people to know. There are plenty of resources to get you started. You can pick up something that you wanted to do all along, or pick up something that is totally unrelated to your field of expertise. This can even double as a new hobby. Numerous online pages and sites offer various activities and courses that you can use to learn something new. It could be a language, calculus, or a new musical instrument—just do something new, and watch you be a better you.

> Believe in possibilities. Believe in human potential. Believe in yourself, and you'll have the power to change your fate.

Day 241: Avoid the Negative

We build relationships from the time we are children till the day we die. As children, we do not know what is good or bad for us and often create relationships that are unedifying and not uplifting. We end up choosing people as friends who pull us down with their negativity and crabbiness. Ever had someone like that in your life? Of course, we all do. Now, here is what you do. Think about such people in your life—those who do not give you any emotional energy but take it away instead. *Keep your distance*, and you'll be happier. Such people are going to be miserable underachievers in the future, who will always complain about life, and they will drag you along with them. It is in your best interest to stay away.

Give to others. Instead of spending time with people like the ones just described, spend it with those who are less fortunate than you. If you have time, you might also want to volunteer at a local charity or nonprofit organization. VolunteerMatch, GiveBack, and AllForGood can help you find one that's right for you. This will not only help you do well for society, but it will change your perspective on life and teach you to be grateful for what you have.

*If your actions inspire others to dream more, learn more,
do more, and become more, you are a leader.*

Day 242: Evaluate, Track, and Enhance

Every few days, it's a good idea to evaluate your life and check if you are where you want to be. There are a few questions you should ask yourself that will help you evaluate what you are doing in life.
First, "Am I doing what I love?" It's hard to be the best version of you if you're not happy with what you are doing with your life. If this was your last day on earth, would you be doing what you are doing today? If not, then maybe you need to think about what you could be doing that would leave you feeling more fulfilled. Come up with a list of activities that will satisfy you and add them to your days so your answer to this question is an affirming yes!
Second, "What's the worst that could happen?" Ever wake up with a sense of impending doom, as if something bad is going to happen? This will hinder your further growth and success. The best thing to do is to ask yourself, "What is the worst thing that could really happen if [insert potential future bad situation here] were to come true?" In other words, if you truly think through potential situations and their outcomes, you'll likely see that most aren't a life-or-death deal.
Finally, "What good have I done today?" Always end the day with this question. This simple question at the end of your day provides you with an opportunity to reflect and gives you perspective. It forces you to consider whether you're heading in the direction you want to go and to take others into account.

> The will to win, the desire to succeed, and the urge to reach your full potential...these are the keys that will unlock the door to personal excellence.

Day 243: Stacking Habits

Kaizen, a Japanese word meaning "continuous improvement," is often applied in business situations to improve how a business runs and, therefore, the profitability of the entire operation.

More often than not, we all have been guilty of failing at our new habits that we would like to have built up. And that is because of a couple reasons, such as trying too much too early. "I will do one hundred pushups from tomorrow." Wham! That is the sound of your plan falling like a pack of cards. A better idea would be to try the "five-minute rule."

You can do most anything for five minutes—run, sing, or practice the piano, for example. Five minutes. That's like peanuts. If you can set this time aside, by the time the five minutes are up, you will be so "into" the activity that quitting will be tough. So stop aiming high. Just aim for five minutes and watch your life change.

Another reason we fail is that we don't stack our habits up or use triggers. A plan to do something at the end of the day before going to sleep is bound to fail. Instead, use your newly formed habit and stack this other habit onto it. Let your well-formed habits trigger new ones you want to form. For example, now that you have started exercising regularly, start practicing your guitar immediately after that, or start meditating after your exercise as you cool down. This way, you ensure that both your habits go hand in hand, and you achieve more.

You can't win unless you try. Effort is the only way to get results.

Day 244: Reducing Risk through Multifamily Ownership

Owning a multifamily unit allows you to spread your risk. When you own a single-family home as an investment, you depend on the income of one individual or one family for the money to pay your mortgage and expenses each month. But what if Mr. Tenant stumbles home late one too many times, and Mrs. Tenant finally says she's through? Any change in one household's financial status (including loss of a job, a debilitating injury, divorce, or death) can throw your ability to meet your mortgage obligations into a tailspin. In addition, a departing family leaves the vacant property vulnerable to everything from break-ins to vandalism to busted pipes in winter until you're able to find new tenants. A building housing multiple families increases the chances that you will have some amount of income at all times.

Your life is a product of your decisions. Make the ones that matter.

Day 245: Rolling Out the Red Carpet for First-Time Homebuyers

Property owners boost the national economy. They pay property taxes and spend money at home-improvement stores. Owners also stabilize communities by reducing resident turnover and crime rates. No wonder both the federal government and private lenders pull out all the stops to encourage renters to take the leap. Many loan programs cater to first-time homebuyers by offering lower down payments, lower interest rates, and lower credit-score requirements. Some institutions even allow you to requalify as a first-timer. If a certain number of years have passed since you were a legal owner, you might be able to reclaim the status of first-time homebuyer. Grab your superhero cape and step up to receive all the goodies that are waiting for you. And why stop there? Get more bang for your buck by becoming the first-time buyer of a multifamily unit. Owner heroes should be rewarded.

You're better than you were yesterday. You're older, wiser, and more experienced than you've ever been before.

Day 246: Gaze into Your Investing Future with Predictive Technology

What if you had a crystal ball to see when an owner was planning to sell his or her home—long before it ever went on the market? Would you believe this technology already exists? Services like SmartTargeting use algorithms and other predictive analytics to create a targeted marketing system for real estate professionals. Systematic prospecting and technologically advanced farming turn the old days of blind mass mailings into quaint nostalgia. "Big data" algorithmic models create educated projections about which homeowners are likely to sell in the near future. These systems can also generate property-specific info, such as expected appreciation and cash flow, to rate the long-term profitability of a particular property. Get the edge. Be first in line to buy a great investment property before the next investor even knows it'll be available.

Nothing great happens overnight. Work and patience are your friends.

Day 247: Crime Prevention through Environmental Design (CPTED)

In good economic times and bad, crimes against people and property are an age-old concern for those who live in large cities. Experts began to focus more on solving these issues during the early 1960s. They speculated that residential areas are less safe when physical layouts are not thoughtfully considered and when neighbors don't meaningfully interact with one another. Community residents and urban-planning professionals looked for ways to reduce opportunities for crime. Formal guidelines known as crime prevention through environmental design (CPTED) were introduced in the 1970s to deter crime by making certain areas unattractive to criminals. CPTED initiatives include such small changes as planting the right shrubs for visibility and adding park benches for residents to socialize, all the way through large-scale architectural changes for laying out entire communities. Consider how CPTED principles affect the level of safety when choosing where to invest.

Become intentional.

Day 248: Historic Homes as an Investment

Historic homes are deemed historic or "architecturally significant" by the National Register of Historic Places—or by the local historic board—if they exemplify a signature architectural style, capture the essence of a given time period, or are associated with famous people from the past (like my house will be in the future—just kidding). They may also include homes located in neighborhoods designated as historic districts. Now, historic homes are alluring, charming, and easy to fall in love with. However, they can be "white elephants"—they can cause unnecessary expenses and have unnecessary restrictions. Their charm may come with a price. These buildings may have structural problems due to old age, and there may be strict guidelines for rehabilitation that need to be followed. However, it is not all gloomy and dark. There is a bright side to buying historic homes. The aesthetic beauty of historic homes attracts buyers—the buildings have stood the test of time, and their architecture has a charm that is not found in buildings of our era. Many states and local governments offer tax incentives such as tax credits or lower-interest loans for preserving and restoring historic structures. You need to qualify for these tax abatements, but they may be an added perk in going after historic homes.

Believe in yourself and all that you are; know that there is something inside you that is greater than any obstacle.

Day 249: Tips on Buying Historic Homes

Historic homes have an allure and charm that is not present in the houses of this era. Although they may have added perks in the form of tax benefits, you need to be aware of a few things if you are considering buying a historic house. Get a formal home inspection by a qualified home inspector who is an expert in older homes. Get price estimates from contractors regarding all necessary repair work. Ensure that the house meets safety and health standards, including asbestos and lead-paint tests. If there are major structural problems, it's better to walk away. In business, a broken heart is less painful than a recurring headache (only in business, though). Carefully study the standards for rehabilitation of historic buildings imposed by local/state laws for owners of historic structures. There are remodeling requirements that you may not be able to fulfill.

The goal of historic-home renovation is to preserve the home's true nature and original construction (makes sense—who wants to refurbish an old, charming home into a modern architectural disaster?). All owners who wish to renovate must obtain special permits that are subject to restrictions aimed at protecting the essence of the property or neighborhood. Generally, homeowners cannot add footage to these homes, including extra stories. Windows, shutters, and roofs are important in preserving the original style of design. Thus, unless you replace them in kind, you cannot replace the windows. Needless to stay, recreating the old style of windows can be expensive. Yes, there may be tax benefits, but tax levies for merely living in a historic neighborhood may be higher than those in other neighborhoods. Heating or cooling a historic home may cost more than usual. Check out previous years' energy bills. Once you have down your homework, you can take pride in your work and reap the benefits.

Each morning we are born again. What we do today is what matters most.

Day 250: Fixed Costs: What Are They?

Fixed costs are the costs that are fixed for every property you own and plan to sell; you must figure out these costs as accurately as possible and factor them in while trying to deal in real estate. Dealers who don't have an idea of these costs may soon regret it. Remember that failing to plan is planning to fail.

Fixed costs consist of all the various costs, commissions, and fees associated with all parts of the investment project, excluding the actual rehab costs. Fixed costs can be divided into three categories: purchase costs, holding costs, and selling costs. Purchase costs consist broadly of inspection costs, closing costs, and lender fees. There may be other recurring purchase costs, such as appraisal fees, survey costs, bird-dog fees, and so forth; if so, add those into your purchase costs. Holding costs generally include things like mortgage payments, utility payments, and insurance. These are costs incurred during the rehab phase. Selling costs include fees and commissions paid to sell the property, such as agent commissions, closing costs, the home warranty, the termite letter, and MLS fees.

> Take risks—if you win, you will be happy; if you lose, you will be wise.

Day 251: Purchase Costs

Purchase costs are those fixed expenses that are incurred during the purchase of a property, such as inspection costs. If you develop a good working relationship with a property inspector, you may be able to reduce these costs. Closing costs are another category within purchase costs. Each purchase has a fixed set of closing costs paid by the buyer. In Georgia, for example, this includes a title search, lawyer fees, courier fees, recording fees, taxes, and document-review fees. Yet another category is lender fees. Lenders charge fees to fund loans; these fees include a loan origination fee and an appraisal underwriting fee. In this case, again, if you have a lender with whom you work consistently and have a good relationship with, you may be able to negotiate a lesser cost. You also have to factor in other recurring purchase costs, such as appraisal fees, survey costs, bird-dog fees, and so forth, which need to be included in purchase costs. Purchase costs are the most stable and unchanging of the lot of fixed costs if you have factored in all expenses accurately. They can also be reduced if you develop your interpersonal and bargaining skills.

> No matter how slow you go, you are still lapping everyone on the couch.

Day 252: Holding Costs—What Should Be Included and How to Calculate

Holding costs are those costs incurred from the time of purchase of property to its sale. A template for the breakdown of these costs is as follows:

- *Mortgage Payments.* Let's say you take six months to sell off a property with a mortgage that costs $400 each month; your total cost of the mortgage is $2,400. Figure out your approximate duration to sell a property, determine mortgage costs, and come up with as accurate a figure as possible.
- *Property Taxes.* Calculate the property taxes for your area and the amount of time your property is going to be under your care. Calculate the tax accordingly, and factor that in.
- *Utilities.* This includes electricity, water, and gas. A few landowners start running these right after purchase for two reasons: (a) for the convenience of the contractors and (b) to diagnose problems with the property.
- *Insurance.* The longer the property is going to be under your ownership, the higher is this cost.

Other costs may include lawn mowing, snow removal, and similar services. Holding costs is that one area where you may actually miss out on a few points and end up paying extra, so carefully work out the costs incurred here. Try to maximize estimated costs so that you are prepared for every contingency with no last-minute surprises.

It always seems impossible until it's done.

Day 253: Tips for Finding Your Next Investment Property

So you have made a couple of first sales, and now you have reached a dead end. How do you find your next investment property? Here are a few tips. Browse expired listings, and make an offer directly to the owner of the property or to the agent. An offer of 20 to 25 percent below the last listed price is a good deal for them. Properties that have not been sold on the MLS may have owners willing to sell. The offer opens up negotiations and is made before the property is seen. Review the length of time the property has been on the market and how often the price has been reduced. Read the remarks section of the listing. Talk to the agent and find out why the property didn't sell to determine if there are any problems with the property or the seller. Gain insight about the motivation of the seller. The agent has no further obligation to the seller of an expired listing and is more likely to give you some inside information. Expired listings, canceled listings, and entry-only listings can give good yields. Public records will have all the clues. Properties that have no recorded sales in the past thirty years are usually owned by seniors and are passed on from generation to generation; also, they are usually mortgage-free and thus can offer a good deal.

> Everyone who's ever taken a shower has an idea. It's the person who gets out of the shower, dries off, and does something about it who makes a difference.

Day 254: Use Live Media to Bolster Your Business

Let's face it: if you have a self-run business and don't use social media or don't intend to use it yet, then you have been living under a huge rock. Live media can make your property look gorgeous or make your business drop dead if not done properly. Hence, it's time to master this art. Here are a few tips:

1. Walk through your listings. Stroll through your existing listings and show your online audience what your homes look like.
2. Provide neighborhood tours. If you don't have any current listings, then choose a sunny day and walk your viewers through the neighborhood where you usually sell houses, showing some landmarks and offering them some context to the neighborhood.
3. Conduct client interviews. Show your followers how happy your clients are with you and your work.
4. Join community meetups. Organize get-togethers featuring the brightest business minds in your area, such as potluck dinners and bake sales at the local community center.
5. Eat at great restaurants. Good food plays a soft role in attracting tenants. Show off the fine dining available in your property area and highlight the best dishes and wines available locally.
6. Local sightseeing. Forget the fact that you are in the housing market, and think of common local tourist sites that visitors who head to your area would love to see.

Although the world is full of suffering, it is also full of the overcoming of it.

Day 255: Live Social Media Tips

Here are some tips for improving your live social media presence:

- *Staging homes for sale.* Work with professional home stagers who can provide you with tips and tricks to make your listings an emotional hit with buyers.
- *Showcasing life at the office.* Show off your fun side to buyers and followers by highlighting office parties.
- *Giving advice to home sellers.* These are the posts that will grab the maximum eyeballs. Use this to your advantage.
- *Offer expert home-buying tips.* Share the secrets of buying a home with your audience. You have inside information and will be able to guide them through all the pitfalls.
- *Sharing big announcements.* Big life events, such as marriages and births, should be shared with followers because it helps them relate to you and helps them remember you.
- *Answering questions from leads.* Conduct Q&A sessions with your followers. Ensure that you give them enough time to have their questions ready. Set firm start and end times. If they overshoot the time limit, they can contact you in person via e-mail or phone.
- *Sharing a skill or hobby.* Share a skill that can aid your followers, such as business organization skills. Or share something fun, like guitar-playing tips or football skills—anything to make you stand out in a crowd.
- *Telling personal/professional stories.* Storytelling is a lost art. Tell your story with intrigue over live media. If you are able to connect with your followers, you'll watch your market grow.

- *Spending time with family and friends.* An occasional spontaneous live stream of you spending time with loved ones can help you come across as personable and relatable. Please, though, show stuff that your audience will find useful and/or entertaining—long, boring wedding videos are a no-no!
- *Hosting contests and giveaways.* Host a contest to bolster brand engagement and grow your audience. The prize need not be something major.

Do more of what makes you happy.

Day 256: How to Use Other Businesses and Your Audience to Boost Sales via Live Media Apps

So your live media app is up and running well and has a significant number of followers. Now how do you use other businesses, landowners, and your audience to bolster your following on the media app? Don't shy away from getting other landowners in on this by fearing competition. Here are a few ideas on using other real estate professionals in your live media apps:

- Your audience may want to know what local and national pundits have to say about the state of the residential-sector markets. Use this to your advantage by hosting some of these on your site—with the speaker's permission, of course.
- Use your networking skills and contacts as an investor and find individuals who are experts in the field of real estate to interview through live-streaming apps.
- Use connections with locally based entrepreneurs and executives and chat with them to gain insights into how they run their businesses.
- Capture memorable moments at company outings, such as picnics and dinners. Humanize your brand and show your audience that you are approachable and transparent.
- Learn to share the stage with fellow agents at your firm because they may specialize in some matters that could help your audience.
- All of us have great sounding boards to discuss ideas, but occasionally a fresh perspective from outside your social circle can help you brainstorm ideas for improving your brand (e.g., ask opinions on logos, colors, or other visual themes).

- Give positive reviews about local businesses in the community. Use your connections with other businesses, and give them positive reviews, and ask them to return the favor as well. Remember that you need to be credible, so your reviews should not be fake or spurious.

Well done is better than well said.

Day 257: What Is Hard Money?

"Yes, yes—I know what hard money is." Isn't that what you plan to tell me? "It's money that is hard money as opposed to hereditary wealth." Ha! Gotcha! Thanks for letting me know that you don't know. Hard money is an asset-based loan from nontraditional sources (read: *banks*) that relies more on the strength of the real estate purchase than the borrower's financial credentials. Hard-money lenders may be nontraditional, but they are still organized and licensed to loan cash. They have lending criteria. Their loans have defined durations, interest rates, and up-front points. These are well known prior to loan issuance and help the borrower choose the lender. Lending, interest rates, and loan duration all have limits, but they are still negotiable. An agreement that is suitable to all parties will suffice. Hard-money loans are rigid and more expensive. Most hard-money lenders get their funds (partly, at least) from private sources, so they have to increase their interest rates and fees to make a profit. So remember that if you eliminate the middle man, you can cut yourself a better deal. Hard money is usually easier to find because hard-money lenders are in the business of lending. Thus, they tend to advertise their loans. This makes it easier to find them. So, if you are looking for alternative sources of loans, consider hard-money lenders. Their advantages are easy to find, but be prepared to pay for the convenience.

You were given this life because you are strong enough to live it.

Day 258: A Primer on Private Money

Isn't all money private? Well, yes, it is—but that's not what I'm talking about here. This is an asset-based loan from nontraditional sources (read: *banks*) that relies more on the strength of the real estate purchase than the borrower's financial credentials. Private lenders are, well, private. It might be a friend, family member, or colleague, or perhaps just a professional referral. However it may work, their role is strictly based on your agreement with them.

Private money is much more flexible on defined durations, interest rates, and up-front points. Most private loans have no preset criteria, and the loan terms you work out are based purely on your negotiating skills. Private money is more flexible—and usually cheaper! If you compare it with hard money, private money has the primary advantage of flexibility. The only caveat is that lenders are not advertising that they have money to lend. But if you make the effort, private money is available. It is out there to be taken advantage of. It is comparable to hard money, and it is a completely feasible way to fund your real estate deals. The only disadvantage is the lack of awareness about private money.

To be successful you must accept all challenges that come your way. You can't just accept the ones you like.

Day 259: Three Documents That Tenants Use to Scam Unsuspecting Landlords

Scams are everywhere—especially in the digital era. And if that scam can put a roof above one's head, then why not? Three documents are often faked by applicants so that you will accept them as tenants. There is no such thing as a too-thorough background check. Beware of these scams:

1. *The clean credit report.* In this era of computers, even someone with few skills and a fossilized computer that belongs in a museum can use Photoshop to create a fake credit report. They can use someone else's report and use Photoshop to replace the name on the report. That same document can be duplicated and sent to many landlords. All it takes is one gullible landlord to make this scam work. You don't want to be the one.
2. *The fake proof of residence and employment.* Here you have to be smart. There is a market for fake pay stubs—and it is not even illegal to buy or sell them! Applicants will produce fake papers stating employment and residence, with salary slips as proof. So you need to be one step ahead when you call up this "earlier landlord." Ask for some nonexistent person. If you simply ask, "Are you Mr. Smith's landlord?" of course the person will say yes. He has been waiting for your call.
3. *Oversized "employer's checks."* This one is a simple yet brilliant idea that often worked in the last decade—till everybody wised up to it. You receive an e-mail from a wannabe tenant who seems aboveboard, stating that he or she is being asked to move by his or her employer and is being reimbursed for the move. The

wannabe tenant then sends you a check from the fake employer that is for more than the rent/deposit amount. The wannabe tenant then asks you to cash the check and send the extra amount back to someone else. But the check was never real! You end up losing all the money you sent.

> Don't think about what can happen in a month. Don't think about what can happen in a year. Just focus on the twenty-four hours in front of you, and do what you can to get closer to where you want to be.

Day 260: Tantalizing Scams That Your Tenants Could Attempt

In the African jungle, as an old saying goes, a gazelle wakes up thinking that he must outrun the fastest lion to survive. In the same jungle, a lion wakes up thinking that he must outrun the fastest gazelle to survive. The same thing is true in our country—crooks wake up thinking of ways to outsmart the honest, and the honest wake up thinking of ways to not get outsmarted by the cons. Here are two scams that the crook who has his eyes on your money may be using to bamboozle you:

1. *The six-month advance sublet.* This is a dastardly scam because it scams both you and your tenant. You are paid a month's advance rent by your tenant. You go to collect your second month's rent, but you find someone else, whom you never met or knew of, who says that he or she has already paid six months of rent in advance. Basically, the person you dealt with faked owning your property, advertised it as his or hers, rented it to the current tenant by taking six months of rent from him or her, and disappeared. When you go to collect rent, you see an unchecked, unknown tenant who has already paid six months of rent and who can't pay for the second month. Horror of horrors! The only way to avoid this is going through every application with a fine-tooth comb. Remember that in this business, no background check is enough. You have to put in the hard yards for every tenant, every time.
2. *Up-front cash.* If someone offers you six months of rent in hard cash for an immediate move-in, there is only one sound that

should be heard—that of the door slamming in his or her face. Anybody who tries to make you skip the screening process should get that response. Acquiring one-time money is very easy for a criminal. Forewarned is forearmed.

> The man who moves a mountain begins by carrying away small stones.
>
> —Confucius

Day 261: Anatomy of a Rental Scam

Scammers are the scavengers in any successful business. They take someone's hard work and try to use it for their selfish benefit. So how do these scammers function? They might list properties that are not theirs on some Internet listing sites. They might take an existing posting and put it at a different rate or repost sold properties. They might also use listing-management tools to post it across many different sites, awaiting a response. Once contacted, they demand money for the property via MoneyGram or Western Union—*urgently*. That's when you should smell a rat. Personal contact is avoided on excuses as flimsy as a heroine's nightgown. Trulia is committed to maintaining quality by eliminating frauds. Immediate action and continuous improvement is the secret of Trulia's success—the company has a dedicated team and resources to weed out the scavengers.

> I never could have done what I have done without the habits of punctuality, order, and diligence, and without the determination to concentrate.
>
> —Charles Dickens

Day 262: How to Avoid Being Scammed

Nobody is immune to a scam. Here are a few tipoffs in sniffing out a scam:

- The owner urgently demands cash via MoneyGram or Western Union before you have seen the property.
- The owner cannot meet you personally and gives some lousy excuse, which should raise your antennae.
- The listing uses poor grammar, has typos, or gives a long sob story. I smell a rat!

A golden rule in life very true here is that if it seems too good to be true, then it probably is. There are no freebies in life. The following tips will also help protect you from scammers:

- Always visit a property or meet with the owner with another person, such as a friend.
- Google the e-mail address and phone number of the owner. You may see that the owner has already been reported.
- Do not share personal details unless the genuineness of the property has been confirmed.
- Never send money to anybody without securing a lease.
- If you have been duped, contact the local authorities immediately.

No matter how you feel, get up, dress up, show up, and never give up.

Day 263: E-Signatures for Real Estate Documents

You don't want to spend an eternity on your real estate documents—just sign them and move on. This is exactly what DocuSign does. DocuSign allows you the unique and free opportunity to sign and upload a document. All your real estate contracts, forms, and transactions can be signed, sent, and returned in minutes. DocuSign's eSignatures and DocuSign Transaction Rooms make saving to the Cloud simple. DocuSign enables you to add convenience and efficient service for your real estate transactions. Add the ability to sign, send, and manage documents from your desktop or on the go from your mobile devices. You can sync accounts with zipForm Plus, Google Drive, and Dropbox Handle and work with any file type—PDF or Word.

Whatever you can do, or dream you can, begin it.

Day 264: The New Main Street

Investment opportunities in a new style of commercial development are arising in the wake of the overall decline of the suburban shopping mall. Rising gas prices and hectic schedules make driving from store to store less appealing as shoppers gravitate toward a "park once" retail design. More people are turning to the Internet for purchases as the convenience of online shopping increases in popularity. Despite the benefits of online shopping, retail experts agree that the desire of shoppers to visit brick-and-mortar stores in some form will never go away. The difference is that consumers demand more distinctive retail developments that encourage shoppers to linger and stay awhile. Main streets, town centers, and mixed-use development projects are reflecting changing consumer tastes and economic conditions, especially in urban areas. Investors with an interest in commercial real estate might consider learning more.

You only fail when you stop trying.

Day 265: Bright Spots in the Shopping Mall Industry

There's a bright spot in an area of real estate that has seen challenges and declining growth. Although shopping malls in general have faced challenges, owners of upscale shopping malls are seeing growth in their industry. These make up about 40 percent of the nation's malls and have seen improving business in the last few years since the recession. Owners of midlevel strip malls also have some options to remain viable in a changing market. Opportunities exist to lure clients with a need for large commercial spaces, such as health-care facilities, discount retailers, educational institutions, movie theaters, restaurants, and business offices. Larger interior spaces can also be subdivided into smaller spaces to create the perfect fit for specialty stores catering to smaller niche markets.

Do what you have to do until you can do what you want to do.

Day 266: Serving the Needs of the "Medtail" Community Benefits Commercial Landlords

Two converging factors in American society have led to some exciting opportunities for hard-hit landlords who own shopping centers and related commercial spaces. The Affordable Care Act has created a huge surge in patients with insurance looking for services. At the same time, overbuilding and the recession have left vacant many commercial spaces formerly occupied by big-box stores that have gone out of business. A major trend is under way toward repurposing these spaces to fit the needs of the medical retail, or "medtail," community. These arrangements benefit commercial landlords by filling vacant spaces, and they serve health-care provider companies by eliminating the need to build new facilities from the ground up. Property owners must be mindful of certain challenges, such as locating restaurants with strong food odors away from the sensitive noses of patients undergoing treatment. Ultimately, however, the benefits tip the scales toward the owners.

Don't give up. Normally it is the last key on the ring that opens the door.

Day 267: One Tax-Free Property, Two Tax-Free Properties, Three...

Pleasant thoughts of Section 1031 of the Internal Revenue Code have lulled many a smiling real estate investor to sleep. Sweet dreams of counting the tax-free properties they can buy replace the need for counting sheep. Commonly known as the 1031 Exchange, there is a particular type of real estate transaction that allows you to buy and sell properties while avoiding paying taxes. This helps to accelerate the growth of your portfolio by getting more bang for your buck. The way it works is the IRS allows you to take 100 percent of the proceeds from the sale of one property and reinvest those funds into the purchase of another property. The magic words are *tax-free*. Of course, there are certain guidelines, and some restrictions apply, but this loophole has created generations of wealthy investors. Maybe it's time to start *your* family's tradition.

When life puts you in tough situations, don't say, "Why me?" Say, "Try me."

Day 268: Show the Calmness of Mr. Spock

Being a good landlord is much more than just being proficient about technical things such as lease renewals, security deposit interest, and regular maintenance. Don't forget about your interpersonal dealings with tenants. Try to maintain a professional demeanor at all times, even in situations where the tenant appears agitated or irate. *Never get into a shouting match with a tenant*—especially if it appears that the tenant is trying to push your buttons. If the tenant is sincerely upset, he or she will respect and appreciate that you didn't respond in kind once the crisis cools down. If the tenant is trying to provoke an angry reaction from you, never give the tenant ammunition to use against you later. Outbursts by you could be used to reflect negatively on you if the situation ever lands in court. Always be friendly and fair, but remain objective.

Be stronger than your strongest excuse.

Day 269: Avoiding Burnout: For the Landlord's Convenience

Being a landlord is the same as being the owner of a small business. Customer service (or tenant service) should be a priority. Keep in mind that to build a strong business, though, you have to make things convenient for yourself as well. Hold open houses to overlap tenant showings as opposed to individual appointments. Pass on your costs for running background checks and credit checks by charging application fees. Don't hand over the keys to a new tenant until the check has cleared. When it's time to collect rent, avoid running all over town chasing payments. Accept mail payments or online payments only. Maintaining a high level of service to your tenants requires making the best use of your limited time and energy. Avoid landlord burnout for the long-term sustainability of your business.

Nothing can dim the light that shines from within.

Day 270: You Never Get a Second Chance to Make a First Impression

When prospective tenants view your unit, you listen to what they say and the tone they use. You pay attention to how they're dressed and the condition of their clothing. You might even glance into their vehicles to gauge what type of people they are. Did you ever consider that you might be on the receiving end of the same type of silent interrogation? Your meeting with a prospective tenant takes place outside of a workplace in an informal setting. Keep in mind, though, that some of the same expectations of a job interview come into play. The person "holding the chips" is still expected to display a presentable look and demeanor. Well-qualified tenants know they have options. It is as important for the landlord to impress the prospect as it for the prospect to impress the landlord.

Nothing holds you back more than your own insecurities.

Day 271: Give Respect to Get Respect

Property owners have a right to expect respect from people who rent their units. This is displayed in the form of avoiding damage to the unit, paying rent on time, and allowing other residents the quiet enjoyment of their own units. Earn this respect by showing respect in return. A major frustration reported by many tenants is trouble reaching their landlord in a timely manner. If your work schedule prevents frequent personal calls, be up-front about it. Determine a certain window of time (e.g., four hours) during which you can commit to returning a resident's phone call. Let tenants know what they can expect. Try to also have a backup phone number just in case the resident is unable to reach you (or the property manager) at the primary number. Show residents you feel it's important for you to be accessible.

Life is like a camera—you focus on what's important, capture the good times, develop from the negative, and if things don't work out, take another shot.

Day 272: Blocking Problem Tenants in Their Tracks

Having "bad tenants" is one of the major concerns of current and prospective landlords. The best way to deal with problem tenants is to make sure that they don't even cross your threshold. First, you need to decide what type of tenants you're looking for so you'll know them when you see them. Are they students, tradespeople, professionals, singles, or families? Next, you want to figure out where your ideal tenants congregate. Areas that cater to people with a regular income such as gyms or shopping malls are the best choice. Specifically advertise in those areas. Inform applicants that you check references and credit. Explain the lease terms and expectations up-front, including an automatic annual rent increase. Landlords are prohibited by law from unfair discrimination, but advertising your unit to your target market is considered a best business practice.

Almost every successful person begins with these two beliefs: the future can be better than the present, and I have the power to make it so.

Day 273: All Due Respect to the Rehab Process

The reality TV shows paint a fairytale picture of what it's like to buy a dump one day and turn it into a cash cow just a few weeks later. Don't underestimate the rehab process, though. It's an operation that involves legal factors, insurance aspects, potentially dangerous materials and situations, and potentially thousands of your valuable dollars. It does not mind biting the hand that feeds it. If you don't give the process the respect it deserves, it can turn on you like a rogue hamster. Even when you create the most detailed plan, make sure to leave room to deal with inevitable unexpected issues as they arise. Having experienced people on your team, such as a real estate attorney, insurance agent, and contractor, can help you make sure your project is not derailed by contingencies. There's more to rehabbing than just being a good investor.

> If we wait until we're ready, we'll be waiting for the rest of our lives.

Day 274: Not for Personal Enjoyment

Plush carpeting. An in-ground sprinkler system. Top-of-the-line, stainless-steel appliances. Newly installed hardwood floors. You always dreamed of how you would deck out your first property. As a youth, you couldn't wait to grow up to apply the old saying "Your home is your castle." But remember, a rehab is not your home. Before you purchase any materials or give a second look to any fancy upgrade, you must first determine if the market will bear it out. Whether you're fixing a property to flip it or you're buying it and holding it as a rental, you have to make sure that the way you rehab the property will allow for a return on the money you put into it. Never start a rehab project without a detailed budget, and stay within that budget to protect your profits.

Every day may not be good, but there is something good in every day.

Day 275: Create Your Entire Rehab Timeline—before You Start

There's more to a rehab project than swinging a hammer, and it doesn't end when you drive in the last nail. Develop your entire timeline from start to finish before you even begin. Find out before you buy the property how long you might have to hold it before you can refinance your loan for better terms, or before a buyer's lender will let them purchase it from you (called the "seasoning period"). Will you advertise the property for sale or rent before construction is completed? This leaves room for prospective buyers to suggest personal preferences on finishing touches, which might lead them to purchase. Or will you wait until the project is broom clean to market it because you don't trust buyers or renters to use their imaginations? Either way, have a list of prospectives lined up in advance.

Be somebody who makes everybody feel like a somebody.

Day 276: Keep Your Business Straight With Google Keep

While there are many organization apps and apps in the style of Post-it Notes, this app is essential for Google users and enticing for anyone looking for a clean interface to set reminders. Google Keep lets you create Post-its for exactly what you need to remember. You can choose between simple text or a list style for each note. Additionally, you can color-code notes, which is especially useful if you're using the color-coding feature in Google Calendar. The archive feature makes it easy to recall previously set reminders. Best of all, you can set alarms for each note as well as share the notes with other users.

If you can't stop thinking about it, don't stop working for it.

Day 277: The Cornerstone

Change can be the cornerstone of your investment career. Being a successful investor is the foundation of your future. To begin your journey, make a plan. Plan to implement the necessary changes to your lifestyle. Find groups that will contribute to your education. Develop a detailed task list, and implement milestones to measure your achievement. Locate your mentors by carefully validating that they have the experience you need. Be sure your mentors share successful implementation in the specific areas you are targeting for your real estate portfolio. Verify that your definitions of integrity are aligned. Begin doing the hard work. Expect to put in long days as you transition from your existing career and immerse yourself in study for your new goals. Find the books, journals, and publications you need to read. Volunteer to work on the many small tasks that will benefit your mentor. Ask questions as you complete the tasks to find out what is the most efficient style and why. Repeat the process by getting involved with as many experiences as you can.

There is only one way to avoid criticism: do nothing, say nothing, and be nothing.

—Aristotle

Day 278: Your Communication Solution

Start sending an e-newsletter. If you haven't already, you are missing a free interaction with your tenants per month. MailChimp is a web-based e-mail marketing service, and it's free if you keep your list of subscribers to less than two thousand. It has a clean, simple, easy-to-use interface. MailChimp is loaded with a wide variety of customizable templates for designing polished e-mails to get you started. Add your logo and get ready to engage and ignite your residents. Consider embedding a monthly tip on maintenance with a link to live video. Keep a spot reserved for bonus dollars for successful referrals. Add a link to a prequalify form for new applicants. Consider featuring fun neighborhood destinations and current events. Add a Q and A section for residents, and post a common question each month. Reach out to local businesses to feature a coupon. It might even be most helpful to use the scheduling feature to arrive on the twenty-eighth of each month, a most helpful way to get attention on the first.

You can never cross the ocean unless you have the courage to lose sight of the shore.

Day 279: How Do We Rate?

SurveyMonkey is an online survey-development, Cloud-based tool. SurveyMonkey provides free, customizable surveys, as well as a suite of paid back-end programs that include data analysis, sample selection, bias elimination, and data representation tools. If you have kept up your communications, then online surveys are your next step to great property management. What do your customers think of their experience with your office representatives and your maintenance contractor team? Were their expectations for timely professional communication met? Design short surveys to establish a flow of feedback throughout the term of the lease. This feedback ensures your business is running at optimal efficiency and helps to quickly identify areas that need improvement.

I never lose—either I win or I learn.

Day 280: Go Viral On YouTube

YouTube is a video-sharing website owned by Google. Consider the positive impact you can have with your residents by starting a vlogging site. Can you make rules fun? Then consider starting your own channel, and let the fun begin. If you decide to use vlogging, start out by planning what five essential streams of information you need to share. Consider filming places of interest in the area. Introduce them in person to your barber, drycleaner, and nearby businesses. How about maintenance concerns? You might engage a funny, professional friend to create the don't list of sinks, toilets, and disposals. How many friends have shared how watching a YouTube video helped them solve a technical issue? You may want to add some fun, creative moments to your most routine tasks—add a fun, hipster, and creative approach. Consistency is just as key as engagement. Are you prepared to set a schedule for your vlogs and put videos out on time and on a regular basis? Having a consistent schedule lets your audience know when to tune in and when to expect new videos. This is essential for building a resourceful area for long-term success!

Make yourself a priority once in a while. It's not selfish.
It's necessary.

Day 281: Get My Act Together

Consider a folder for each investor (LLC or partner) you work with. Keep a folder for each address you work with and use a consistent naming convention, so you can quickly find each tenant and lease. Add a folder for each template: checklists, condition-report info, questions to ask tenants, emergency phone numbers, phone numbers of your vendors or the landlord's preferred vendors, and HOA contact info.
Store scanned information, such as instruction manuals for appliances and keycodes for garages. Store a report with the initial condition of the property, including photos. This will be essential to have with signatures at the meeting to assess the final condition report when the tenant vacates. Store video or audio recordings of notes on the agreed-upon findings and consider tenant permission to be included.

> The three *C*s in life: choice, chance, change. You must make the choice to take the chance if you want anything in life to change.

Day 282: Start Your Library of Files

Create a marketing folder to store attachments for each property: initial marketing (when, where, how much you spent, marketing photos/video), any inquiries, and where they came from (web, sign call, MLS, etc.), showings with dates and times, as well as any issues to be resolved before a prospective tenant moves in. Don't forget to attach all the related files—lease agreements for that particular property, rental applications (with SSN and bank-account info blacked out if you're worried about security), tenant information, receipts, current HOA docs. Lastly, include photos of any issues found at first walk-through, as well as a separate note with photos at final walk-through, so it's easy to spot any discrepancies and address any final issues.

It always seems impossible until it's done.

Day 283: Keystone Habits

Keystone habits control how you work, eat, play, live, spend, and communicate. A very well-known example of a keystone habit is working out. The areas of your life that are impacted after implementing a workout routine—eating, sleep quality, mood, physical health—is proof that a minor change in one aspect of your life can trigger so many other positive changes. Thus, thoroughly identify all the functions and people who will be highly impacted by your proposed real estate investment change of habit. Determine the circle of friends and family who will be most supportive. Having sufficient support before moving forward with real estate investment will help contribute to a winning plan. Those with less faith will either have to be influenced or removed from your plans. This analysis will help you as you move forward to plan out your teams. Use the same strategies of evaluating their reasons and incentives to help you successfully implement your vision.

> I don't want to get to the end of my life and find that I lived just the length of it. I want to have lived the width of it as well.

Day 284: Your Virtual Treasure Chest

Evernote is a visual treasure chest of your files. It stores and combines data spreadsheets, documents, audio files, and images in one easy-to-manage cabinet with the ability to add notes as you go. If you are working with a landlord who owns multiple properties, you can "stack" those properties' notebooks into one big file under that landlord's name, stacking notebooks in a giant accordion file with numerous file folders inside.

Landlord stack with property info is a great organization tool. The stacking feature is useful for breaking a large project into smaller buckets, organizing your work notes under different focus areas, and compartmentalizing your notes so you can easily navigate between them. The good thing about having Evernote notebooks is the ability to share them with anyone else in the office, and it will sync in "real time"—so your assistant or leasing agent can see notes on any property, even if you're out of the office. With too many attributes to list, Evernote is best at being a shared, synced, written, and visual record.

When something goes wrong in your life, just yell, "Plot twist!" and move on.

Day 285: Blast Out Photos for All Your Friends

Instagram is a popular photo- and video-sharing app that allows you to share your images with friends and other Instagram members. The latest version of the app adds new ways to spice up your photos, including a fade feature. It has a post-notification feature to make it easier to see what your friends post. You can add emojis to hashtags to share your photos.

Include Instagram when you send out an image for a home ready for rental. With a snappy photo including a border and a retro filter effect, it can be a fun and appealing additional asset to your social-media campaign. Ordinary, everyday objects in a home can be transformed into works of art in a few moments and then shared with the Instagram members and all your other social-media friends to admire.

*There is no chance, no destiny, no fate, that can hinder
or control the firm resolve of a determined soul.*

Day 286: Research and More Research

While researching income property, consider the following categories:

- neighborhood
- property taxes
- schools
- job market
- crime
- amenities
- building permits
- future development
- number of listings and vacancies
- natural disasters
- rents

It's important that you explore these options very well before making a final decision to buy real estate. Low vacancy rates allow the landlord to raise rental rates, and you can experience poor tenancy when you buy a property in an area populated with students; therefore, do thorough research before making your final decision. Thoroughly research the impact of these factors as you learn about the area.

> A successful man is one who can lay a firm foundation
> with the bricks others have thrown at him.

Day 287: Lordly Tips

The economy seems like it will soon follow the path of the *Titanic*—again ("experts" at it again). In such a scenario, renting houses is a good source of legal income. But ensure that you know the basics before setting sail. Tips to guide you on this voyage include the following:

- *Being a landlord means business.* Yes, this is usually forgotten. Plan well and factor in customers, liabilities, and expenses beforehand. Otherwise your dreams may turn into nightmares.
- *Start small.* Don't buy the *Playboy* mansion straightaway. Test the waters with small houses and with partners, if needed, till you are fine with diving in.
- *Look before you lease.* Don't buy without checking out the locality. If the offer is too good to be true, then it probably is.
- *Count your chickens…and their droppings as well.* Estimate your rent correctly by factoring in local rates and expenses such as maintenance and vacancy periods. Hire a good accountant, if possible (yes, seriously).
- *Learn to be a DIY professional.* Being handy around the house helps—it can save you the added expenses of calling in plumbers, electricians, and other specialists.
- *Be a team player.* Form a team that includes an accountant, a real estate lawyer, and reliable maintenance workers. A property-management committee is handy for day-to-day dealings with tenants, although the final call should always be the landlord's. Needless to say, a thorough background check will avoid unnecessary heartburn and heart attacks later.

- *Keep your tenants happy.* Respect and proper maintenance keep tenants happy, which prevents unnecessary losses due to vacant property. A proper background check for all tenants is crucial.

Success is knowing your purpose in life.

Day 288: Tips on Renting Property

Statistics are like a bikini—they reveal a lot but hide the interesting parts. Getting to know these hidden parts will determine your success in the real estate business. Check out this list:

- *Neighbors.* The neighborhood determines the type of tenants and vacancy periods—Brad Pitt's neighbor isn't going to be your plumber. Calculate your tax liabilities, and research tax rates in various areas. High tax rates may indicate desirable properties.
- *Schools.* If you want families as tenants, the property should be near good schools. Property is valued on the price it fetches.
- *Crime.* Nobody wants to live in areas where crime is rampant. Local crime statistics may tell you which areas to avoid.
- *Job market.* Keep a lookout on the latest job boom. Silicon Alley and Manhattan would be nowhere if there were no houses for employees.
- *Amenities.* There's no point in having a mansion in the middle of the desert. Ensure basic facilities are nearby for easy access.
- *Vacancy rates and listings.* Listings give an idea about seasonal cycles and bad neighborhoods. Vacancy rates directly determine rent rates.
- *Rent rates.* Budget your tax rates and factor future hikes in taxes into your rates—or else you will be caught with your pants down.
- *Natural disasters.* Getting insured is a smart idea if the area is prone to disasters, such as earthquakes, floods, or Bieber concerts.

> Be miserable. Or motivate yourself. Whatever has to be done, it's always your choice.
>
> —Wayne Dyer

Day 289: No Love at First Glance

So you have refused a property because it looks ugly. The wallpaper is peeling off, the roof is leaking, the exterior looks dilapidated, and well, it basically looks like the set for the next James Wan film. But you may lose out on a potential winner there. Here are a few tips to look for the prospective swan among the ugly ducklings:

- *They are a good deal.* Most "ugly" houses come at a cheap price because of low demand. After buying it cheaply, you can owner finance it to a family for maintenance cash flow. This way you have a source of income and a grateful family.
- *Look around you.* OK, so the house looks ugly, but if the neighborhood is good and there are basic amenities around it, such as schools, malls, parks, and hospitals, then renovating the house may be a smart investment.

Next time, remember that beauty is not skin deep. At least in property.
The successful warrior is the average man, with laser-like focus.

—Bruce Lee

Day 290: Real Estate for Smarties

Real estate investment can appear daunting when you are just getting started. Looking at Mt. Everest may seem daunting from base camp, but each small step will draw you closer to the summit. So here are a few tips to help you out on this endeavor:

- *Get started.* A house is your biggest expense (yes, more than your spouse and kids). Hence, it is better to buy one early, no matter how small. Once you have enough money, you can move into a bigger house and rent out your first digs.
- *Bank on the bank.* Most residential financers will give you at the most four, eight, or ten units (more if you are lucky). Just take what you can and work with it. You will be surprised at the result.
- *Be like the tortoise, not the hare.* Slow and steady wins the race. Keep investing consistently. It wins out in the long run, unlike sudden bursts of saving followed by inactive periods.

> Whenever you find yourself on the side of the majority,
> it is time to pause and reflect.
>
> —MARK TWAIN

Day 291: Crowdfunding—Jumping on the Wagon

Crowdfunding is now the "in thing" in investing. But what does it mean? It's just a fancy term for the pooling of money by various people to buy a particular entity and the subsequent sharing of profits. It has powered the boom in apps and start-ups and may well revolutionize real estate investment. Here are some crowdfunding facts:

- *Old wine in a new bottle.* Crowdfunding is not a new idea, but it has been given a definite boost by app-based services and the Internet.
- *Regulatory easing.* As usual, the last people to change are the authorities, who are yet to ease regulations for small investors. However, there are some indications of a changing trend. If this is actually true, then crowdfunding may leap *above* an annual growth of 25 percent.
- *Awareness.* Once regulatory easing occurs, the next focus would be education of the masses, which should not be an issue if one goes by precedents.

Develop success from failures. Discouragement and failure are two of the surest stepping-stones to success.

—Dale Carnegie

Day 292: Do I Really Need an Accountant?

Having an accountant is like having a computer: they're both useless if you don't know how to use them. Here are a few other hats that your accountant should be wearing to ensure your business is in great shape:

- *The tax breaker.* The most basic accountant should be able to help you utilize your tax breaks.
- *The business minder.* Your accountant should proactively look out for ways in which your business can improve. Your business should be your accountant's business. If there is a good deal for you, he or she should be on it.
- *The portfolio reviewer.* Your accountant should review your investment portfolio and provide you with fresh input. Many businesses have gone kaput purely because there was no second opinion. Don't be another casualty.
- *The record keeper.* Your accountant should provide useful tools and checks to manage your property business. The requirements will vary from person to person, but the principle is the same—to help you get the most out of these tools.
- *The networker.* Your accountant should be an able networker who helps you get in touch with useful people in your field, so that your business prospers.

Don't wish it were easier—wish you were better.

Day 293: How to Choose an Accountant

An accountant is a must to help you get good tax breaks and valuable input on your investment portfolio. But there's a reason for those accountant jokes you've heard. You need to be on your toes while choosing one, or else you might soon end up on a shrink's couch. Here are the qualities you need to look for in an accountant:

- *Expert.* Your accountant should be an expert in the field in which you seek his or her expertise. In other words, your accountant should specialize in property clients.
- *Investor.* It would be great if your accountant is involved in property as well. This means he or she understands the business, and the accountant's interests are aligned with yours.
- *Reasonably priced.* Your accountant should help you make and save money, and this won't happen if a large chunk is being gobbled up by your accountant. A highly priced accountant may imply too many clients, which means less personal involvement.
- *Rapport builder.* It is important to trust and have a good rapport with your accountant.

> You must expect great things of yourself before you can do them.
>
> —Michael Jordan

Day 294: How to Choose a Professional Management Company

A professional management company (PMC) is vital for quick and efficient response to tenants. A prompt manager helps retain tenants, whereas a sloppy one can lose even the most loyal of them. Also, a delay in maintenance can lead to escalating costs or lawsuits if there are injuries. A criterion for selecting a company should be a clear policy on response time to complaints, with an emergency response within twenty-four hours. The manager should be a cool and calm communicator and also should be able to separate the wheat from the chaff when it comes to complaints from tenants. Owner and tenant references help in selecting a company, but ensure that you are not swayed by a single review—good or bad. One should get an overall "feel" for a company based on the overall reviews and then only select one.

We will either find a way or make one.

Day 295: How to Be a Student Magnet

Being a landlord is all about relationships. How you handle your student tenants will determine whether your business will flourish or not. Here are a few tips on being student-friendly:

- *Take the initiative.* Most universities conduct property fairs for local landlords where they can showcase their properties and get in touch with students. Think of it as a singles bar for real estate owners.
- *Rent-by-bed, not rent-by-group.* Rent-by-bed is a good way to ensure that each student is responsible for his or her own lease and does not have to pay for someone else's misdeeds. The teetotaler should not get kicked out for the drunkard's behavior.
- *Interior designers.* It is important to account for the needs of students and accordingly design the personal and group space.
- *Be social.* Encourage engagement with the local community by organizing parties or barbeques to keep goodwill in the neighborhood. Be proactive in engaging with the tenants.
- *Be transparent.* This is a relationship, and honesty is a must. This means being transparent in rent rates and your own needs about property maintenance.

> Live as if you were to die tomorrow. Learn as if you were to live forever.
>
> —Mahatma Gandhi

Day 296: How to Get Students Interested

With student housing, a great idea to generate awareness and increase the leads for your property is to host a contest. Contests bring visibility, but if not done well, they can fail. Here are a few tips on succeeding at these:

- *Put some thought into the prizes.* If you are buying a gift for your girlfriend, you will buy something she desires, not what you want to give her. Why do anything else for the contest? Think of something the students would find valuable, and use that as the prize.
- *KISS (keep it simple, stupid).* When enrolling students in the contest, don't behave like a prospective father-in-law by asking too many questions. Instead, entice them, build their interest, and make entry a breeze.
- *Lead generation.* The leads you have generated need to be followed up. Highlight what makes your property stand out, and make them wonder why they have not rented there already.
- *Go online.* That is where the business, money, visibility, and students are. If you're not there, you're missing out on 99 percent of your student market.

What if I told you that ten years from now, your life would be exactly the same?

Day 297: Spaces That Can Be Used to Increase Storage

Whether you are an astronaut, landlord, or a tenant, space matters. Some tenants want a good neighborhood, some want a good view, and some want basic amenities around the property. But *all* tenants want space. As a landlord, this should be your priority. Making space is easy, inexpensive, and convenient. Here are three typical storage spaces that you are probably not utilizing well enough:

- *Closets.* Closets have lots of wasted space above the shelf and along the sides. Installing a closet-organizer system creates more shelf space. These triple the space and help organize it. The space above the shelf can also be compartmentalized with wood or wire.
- *Bathroom cabinets.* Install cabinet organizers, such as wire or wood shelves and dividers, to help your tenants organize their space.
- *Kitchen cabinets.* Kitchens need the maximum storage space, and this can be easily achieved. Some ideas include installing a lazy Susan or two on central shelves, wire shelves, pot-lid holders, door-mounted racks, and tray organizers.

A winner is just a loser who tried one more time.

Day 298: How to Create Storage Space in Atypical Areas

Storage space in atypical areas can impress tenants because it not only caters to their needs but also implies creativity and effort undertaken on their behalf. Here are a few inexpensive ideas for creating storage space in atypical places at your rental property:

- Add a couple of permanent shelves above the toilet in the bathroom.
- Install shelves on the sides of wider bedroom closets.
- Mount behind-the-door organizers on the doors.
- Put sturdy hooks inside pantries, in closets, and on the walls behind bathroom doors.
- Install shelves on the top part of one wall in the garage.

The following ideas can be used if you are willing to spend more cash:

- Cut into short walls to create recessed shelving between the studs.
- Add a small kitchen island with plenty of cabinet space.
- Turn the space under the stairs into a storage compartment.
- Transform unused crawl spaces, odd nooks, and angled empty space into closets or floor-to-ceiling, built-in shelves.
- Purchase a storage shed for the property.

When it comes to storage, it's time for you to let your creative self go free.
Dead last is greater than did not finish, which trumps did not start.

Day 299: Hell Freezes Over

Snow can be a living hell for landlords because tenants injured by slips and falls can sue them. Landlords and tenants should check the lease terms to know who is responsible for snow removal. If it's your responsibility, be sure to do it right, or you'll face potential lawsuits from people who slip. For example, in a case in Illinois, an elderly woman slipped on the topmost stair where the snow had been shoveled only from the center and not at the sides of the staircase. The sides were covered with a foot of snow, and the handrail was inaccessible from the center. She sued the landlord. The court ruled in her favor, stating that the landlord was not obliged to clean the snow according to the law, but because he had undertaken the endeavor, his not doing it properly was the cause of the injury. That's a chilling thought for you to ponder this winter.

> The people who get on in this world are the people who get up and look for the circumstances they want, and if they can't find them, make them.

Day 300: A Walk down Parking Avenue

Parking spots are an excellent way to make extra money from your properties, depending on the neighborhood. In a metro area with limited parking, lease spots to nontenants. When the supply is low and demand is high, you can cash in by charging nontenants a premium for spots. You don't want to lose a good tenant, though, so add a clause in the agreement that allows you to terminate the parking contract with thirty days' notice. Tenants with more cars mean more money. In the suburbs, where overnight parking is prohibited, the first tenant space can be free, but each extra car can be charged fifty dollars per month, for example, if tenants have multiple cars. Also consider providing numbered and premium spots. Assign a numbered spot (or spots) to each unit so that tenants realize they are getting value for their money. Charge a premium for spots closer to the building or for a covered garage.

> Being defeated is often a temporary condition. Giving up is what makes it permanent.

Day 301: Getting Started with Parking Spaces

Treat each parking-lease agreement like an apartment lease. Before renting to a nontenant, have an attorney prepare a parking-lease agreement. Ensure that the contract protects the owner from any liability that may result from accidents, scratches, theft, or vandalism. Ensure that renters have theft insurance. Indoor garages require a tight security policy. When leasing to nontenants, perform background checks, and require a certificate of insurance from renters. Install proper lighting and security cameras as deterrents. Tenants should know the rules in tandem parking agreements. Tenants should be responsible for moving cars and letting one another out. Ensure that this is mentioned in the lease. If your existing spaces are large, convert them into tandem spots. By accommodating multiple cars such as compacts and subcompacts, you could double your parking revenue.

Discipline, not desire, determines destiny.

Day 302: Fixing the Rules on Fixing

How many landlords does it take to change a lightbulb? I don't know the answer, but I'm sure this question struck a chord with a few of you. Fixing things in rented houses can be a problem. It may be the landlord's responsibility to provide a fit and habitable property and maintain appliances supplied as a part of the agreement, but tenants also have a responsibility to keep the place well maintained and not behave as if the house were part of a *Godzilla* film set. Be sure your lease defines what is and isn't covered. Consider adding a repair-cost fee sheet. Develop a list of common problem items and fees. Consider the parts and labor needed for repeated repairs, and proactive regularly scheduled maintenance. Settle these issues beforehand—on paper.

It's wonderful what we can do if we're always doing.

—George Washington

Day 303: The Hard Yards

"No pain, no gain" is an aphorism that rings true even in the real estate business. For some reason, there is a misconception that it's a lie-back-and-watch business. Rubbish. Real estate is back-breaking, butt-kicking work. You need to reinvest your earnings—you cannot just use all your earnings to buy that fancy-looking Mercedes. Real estate requires reinvestment, be it hiring another employee or utilizing the capital for property improvements. Business growth requires money. You must spend time, money, and effort. Yup—it's hard work. If you don't want to put in the hard yards, find another line of work. You must be always willing to evolve; the only thing that is permanent is change. The real estate field is always evolving. The smart ones evolve. The dumb ones, well…ever heard of the dodo? No? That makes sense, because it's extinct. Get the hint.

Thinking will not overcome fear, but action will.

Day 304: How to Write Letters of Intent with Intent

Commercial-property purchasing requires a letter of intent (LOI), which is written prior to a purchase contract and displays interest in the property. The essential aspects of an LOI are as follows:

- *Purchase price.* This should also include the amount you will put down, the earnest-money deposit, and how much you plan to finance, if any.
- *Inspection period/due diligence period (DDP).* Inform the seller of how long you will need to do your due diligence on the property, including inspections, lease audits, review of financials, and so forth.
- *Financing period.* Inform the seller of how long you will need to arrange financing.
- *Earnest-money deposit.* Note how much you are putting down and how soon and information about refunds.
- *Contract to purchase.* Outline how fast the contract needs to be completed.
- *Brokerage fees.* Outline how the commissions are going to be handled if you have a broker.
- *Closing date.* Explain when closing will occur once finances have been secured and the DDP has expired.
- *Closing costs.* Outline how closing costs will be handled.
- *Period of acceptance.* This is the deadline on the seller for accepting your offer.
- *Conditions.* All additional conditions should be addressed up-front to avoid future problems.
- *Signatures.* Make sure you include your signature and the date, and leave a space for the seller to sign and date your LOI for acceptance.

> The only person you are destined to become is the person you decide to become.
>
> —Ralph Waldo Emerson

Day 305: How to Attract Attention

A letter to attract business can be like a car-chase scene in a movie. If done well, it can attract a lot of interest, but if done poorly, it can lead to yawns. To make an impression, you need to be *different* and attract *immediate* attention. How does one do that? Here are some ideas:

- *The personal letter.* Whether it is your wife or your life, nothing works like a bit of personal attention. A personal letter tells the reader you took extra time to write the letter and immediately gives you an edge over competitors.
- *The final notice.* This works mainly with procrastinators. It tells them they need you—*badly*. It instills a sense of urgency.
- *The double-sided letter.* The front side of this letter has a bold statement, and the back side has a request for details.

So what are you waiting for? Get your pen and paper out, and get started!

Through perseverance, many people win success out of what seemed destined to be certain failure.

—Benjamin Disraeli

Day 306: Master Your Postcards

Sending a postcard to get clients can be a hit-or-miss affair. I have had considerable experience in this field and have come up with a few theories that may help you master this issue. But a bit of a disclaimer is warranted: these theories are just that—theories. So there's still a lot of stuff we don't know and need to learn. The letter isn't everything. You need to stand out from the crowd, and for that you need a message that grabs attention like a haymaker on the jaw. If you know the importance of being different, standing out will be easy. Use the trial-and-error method. To master the art of postcard writing, you will have to write different styles of letters and see what works for you. You can try templates, but nothing works like figuring out what draws attention in your area.

No matter how slow you go, you are still lapping everyone on the couch.

Day 307: How to Design a Bandit

Bandit signs are lawn signs used for real estate advertising to let others know you are interested in buying their homes. Having done the groundwork for bandit signs, the next step is to design a good sign. It's best to make two to five hundred signs because a lot will be lost or taken down. A few guidelines you should adhere to are as follows:

- Use an easily memorized, untraceable phone number. Do not put your name or your company's name on the sign.
- Keep the message short and simple, with large, bold font and a matching color scheme.
- If you are a licensed Realtor, make sure to check with your local board of Realtors to see if you need to represent yourself as a licensed Realtor on your signage.
- Create a route map. A route map allows you to track leads and provides an overview of your strategy.
- Track incoming leads. Determine which areas of your route map generate more responses by asking prospective sellers where they saw your advertisement.
- Build a list of buyers. Look for the signs of other buyers and note their contact details for later reference.

It always seems impossible until it's done.

Day 308: How to Implement Bandit Signs

Once you have decided to proceed with bandit signs, it's time to decide on implementation. First, determine your budget and plan. Once you have established the budget, develop a sound marketing plan. Budget according to response rates. Remember, one deal may justify all the expenses, so don't scrimp. Second, know what you will do once you get your leads. Establish the method by which you wish to receive the leads (i.e., calls or e-mails), and create a system for receiving and responding to them. Known as a lead-intake system, this process enables tracking of incoming leads and responses. Incoming deals should not stop you from marketing simultaneously. That's the essence of a successful business. Common lead-intake systems include Google Voice, a free virtual phone service that can redirect calls to a third-party number for you to answer later; call centers, which have live receptionists to answer calls; and website squeeze pages, in which interested parties are directed to a website squeeze page that gives contact details.

It always seems impossible until it's done.

Day 309: Eviction—the Ultimate Test

The handling of an eviction is the ultimate test of a smart landlord. Here are a few tips on how to ace the test and pass with flying colors:

- *Start early.* Don't dillydally. Start the eviction process with a notice at the first default. You can always revoke it if needed.
- *Document everything.* A smart landlord maintains a written record of everything—conversations, notices, letters, and so forth—and maintains it with date and time.
- *Get state specific.* Most landlords know only the general laws, but the devil lies in the details. Knowing your state laws will prevent you from getting into trouble later.
- *Court communications.* Don't just file the first letter with the court and then forget about it. Follow up, talk to the clerk (without being pesky), and keep submitting records as required.
- *Be patient.* Nothing happens in a day. Let your anger go; chasing the tenants can backfire. Let the system do its job.

> Everyone who's ever taken a shower has an idea. It's the person who gets out of the shower, dries off, and does something about it who makes a difference.

Day 310: Why Use Skip-Trace Services?

Skip-trace services are used to find people who have skipped town. Can they be of any use to real estate investors? Well, we're not cops, but there are several reasons for a real estate investment company or individual property investor to use this type of service:

- *Enhance due diligence and screening practices.* Skip-trace services can be used to dig deeper and verify a variety of factors when filtering tenant applications or lease-option homebuyers, and they are useful for checking out new potential vendors, business partners, and new hires.
- *Track absentee homeowners.* Such systems can be used to track absentee homeowners, such as for good properties where the owners have left town and are unlisted. A skip-trace service could help track the owners; it can also help verify who the owner of a property really is.
- *Track down debtors.* Skip-tracing companies may be used to track down debtors who have skipped out on their leases.

Although the world is full of suffering, it is also full of the overcoming of it.

Day 311: Hey, Dog!

Who or what is a real estate dog? He or she is a person who locates either distressed properties or distressed sellers on behalf of another investor. The assistance of a real estate dog is ideal for the inexperienced, cashless individual who can't make his or her own deals. Playing this role is like being a gopher for a local investor and helping him or her get good deals. Before starting out, check out the legalities in your state regarding being paid a "finder's fee." You don't want to get into hot water later because you didn't know the rules. Now, how is this different from being a real estate wholesaler? A wholesaler locates significantly discounted deals, gets them under contract, and then markets them to his or her own list of cash buyers willing to pay more than what the wholesaler got it for. It's the next step after a bird dog; a bird dog is the beginning, like being a paid intern. This is the place where you start your real estate journey.

Well done is better than well said.

Day 312: Sniffing Opportunities as a Bird Dog

Find a local, experienced real estate investor who can train you on the criteria needed to draw in the deals, which mainly include property info and contact information. Be on the prowl. Go on the hunt to uncover good deals. Find interested sellers and distressed properties that fit your seller's desire. Your investor won't pay you for a deal that he or she can easily acquire, so be smart and diligent. Gift wrap it for your boss. Having found a deal, organize things so that they go smoothly for your boss, and the actual deal is a cakewalk. Then you can sit back and let the dough come in. Being a bird dog lets you earn and learn. The best places to start include REIAs and local foreclosure auctions. It's time for the hunt now—happy sniffing!

You were given this life because you were strong enough to live it.

Day 313: Solving the Realtor Conundrum

Realtors are tough to predict—it's hard to tell whether they will be beneficial or harmful. There's one thing that concerns them most: closing. They get paid when a deal occurs. Thus, get to know your realtor as if you are choosing a mate. If you align your incentives (which in both cases are monetary), then both will profit. However, just like finding a partner, this may be tricky and may require time, patience, and a few dates (deals) to clinch the matter. Ask agents to provide a list of what they've listed and sold, with contact information, and ask the agent if anyone was particularly pleased or particularly disappointed with the results. Doing your research will pay off and help to avoid disappointments and miscommunications.

When you are going through hell, keep going.

Day 314: Show Us Your Stuff

There are dozens of amazing real estate listing presentation software options on the market today, but some are too robust with features for the average landlord to consider. An austere platform that can help with comparative market analysis (CMA) presentations is FlowVella. Add images, audio and video clips, and text to slick-looking slides, and share your creation with prospects to win them over and prove you're a modern agent with digital savvy. PowerPoint for the mobile-first generation has now brought its app to the iPhone. As with its tablet counterpart, FlowVella lets you create rich presentations using touches and gestures, while also adding multimedia like GIFs, videos, and audio, as well as PDFs, words, and images, as you could with more traditional desktop-productivity software. In addition, the app makes it easy to pull in content you have saved in the Cloud on services like Dropbox or Box, or you can grab images from Google Image Search or videos from YouTube. Another unique feature that differentiates FlowVella's presentations from legacy-productivity software is that its presentations are meant to be shared as URLs.

Every flower must grow through dirt.

Day 315: Finding Your Waze

Waze is a community-powered mapping and navigation app that gives you real-time traffic information and road alerts. Waze is free and a great app for yourself and your maintenance team, reducing driving time for your team and saving money. What makes Waze such a powerful app is its continuous update of database information. Users are actively contributing to the data points that create accurate maps. Road closures due to extensive construction are accurately represented, and one-way streets and turn restrictions match their real-world correspondents. While it is a fundamental necessity to have accurate mapping, Waze's mastery of the accuracy of its traffic and incident data have won over many loyal landlords. By leaving the app running whenever you drive, you are doing your part in contributing to the overall accuracy of the real-time map and traffic data.

Life starts at the edge of your comfort zone.

Day 316: Invent a Game You Can Win

As the second of ten children, what are your options if you struggled just to make straight Ds in high school, and you passed through twenty jobs by the time you were twenty-three? The *best* option is to use real estate as a tool to become the most well-known and successful name in one of the world's most iconic cities. That's exactly what *Shark Tank*'s Barbara Corcoran, the self-styled queen of the New York market, did. Her determination took her from her humble beginnings in the two-bedroom New Jersey apartment she shared with her siblings to a swanky high-rise home overlooking Central Park. In less than twenty-five years, she was able to sell the tiny real estate firm she started in 1978 with a loan of $1,000 for almost $70 million. If the chips are stacked against you, just invent a new game.

Life isn't about waiting for the storm to pass; it's about learning to dance in the rain.

Day 317: The Landlord's Toy Store

If you haven't established a relationship with your local hardware store, you probably have not rehabbed your first property. This relationship is an important one. Finding ways to save money when purchasing materials is 101 to your investment game. A hardware store provides the primary life-support system to resuscitate your rehab property off the flatline monitor.
Home Depot recognizes this and has worked hard to establish a loyalty program just for you. With sophisticated reporting tools, they know the needs of their investors. You can take advantage of the ability to log and track purchase orders by address or job name. You can approve maintenance-staff purchases with a quick text. Consider using a Pro Xtra reloadable card to limit and track purchases and receive e-receipts of all transactions. You can rely on two years of purchase data for quick access when a replacement item is needed. Manage, analyze, and grow your business with easy-to-use, professional business tools. Knowing what's available will help you establish a strong bond with the hardware store of your preference.

Not everyone will be part of your future. Some people are just passing through to teach you lessons in life.

Day 318: Every Successful Person's Top Goal

It doesn't matter who you are. It doesn't matter where you're from. It doesn't even matter where you want to be and what lifestyle you desire. Every successful person, without exception, must have the same top aim. Your biggest goal in life should be…(drumroll, please) to never stop setting goals. Having goals should never feel like drudgery. In fact, it's the opposite. Often people are the most miserable when life feels the most stagnant, regardless of how much money, fame, or power they have. The human spirit craves challenge and stimulation. One definition of success is "the progressive realization of a worthy goal." That's what life is really all about. True value is found in your journey—not your destination.

Stay humble, work hard, and be kind.

Day 319: The Goal of a Balanced Life

Goal setting applies to anything you consider to be important in your life. Fulfilling your professional and financial plans is important, but only when viewed in the larger context. The big picture includes all those elements that make you a whole person. What about your spiritual, mental, and physical health? How does your family fit into the equation? Set goals for these areas, and make sure they complement one another. If one of your goals is to spend five hours every evening after work learning about real estate, it might not mesh well with your goal to spend more quality time with your family. Find a healthy balance. Recognize that even when your time is divided between different areas of your life, consistent effort will get you where you need to go without sacrificing what matters.

I'm not afraid of change; I'm more afraid of staying the same.

Day 320: Real Estate Requires Money

Real estate requires money, which can be difficult if you are starting out from scratch. It may be costly to operate because property is tangible and requires ongoing maintenance. Real estate requires ongoing management at two levels: the day-to-day functioning, which can be done by you or a property manager, and the long-term strategic position. Both of these require time, research, and money. Even in real estate, it is most beneficial to build a diversified portfolio, which means a variety of locations and a variety of housing types. Like any other asset class, real estate is cyclical. It has two cycles: the leasing-market cycle and the investment-market cycle. The leasing market consists of the market for space in real estate properties. The supply side is the vacancies available, and the demand side is the amount of space required by tenants. So begin your journey knowing your obstacles, and set your course for success.

You must constantly ask yourself these questions: Who am I around? What are they doing to me? What have they got me reading? What have they got me saying? Where do they have me going? What do they have me thinking? And most important, what do they have me becoming? Then ask yourself the big question: Is that OK? Your life does not get better by chance; it gets better by change.

Day 321: Advantages of the Rent-to-Own Option for Investors

There are many options, strategies, and combinations of methods along the spectrum of investing in rental properties. One option that lies somewhere between fixing and flipping and buying and holding is the rent-to-own investment strategy. An advantage over the fix-and-flip strategy is that providing rent-to-own options gives the owner a regular monthly cash flow versus a one-time payout. A major and much-loved advantage over the buy-and-hold strategy is that the responsibility for maintenance and repairs is shifted from the owner to the renter. For buyers, the path to homeownership is shortened because they are not required to wait until their credit profile improves. The ideal rental candidate is able to afford a mortgage. This means that although income is not a barrier, bruised credit might stand in the way of qualifying. The investor benefits by catering to this niche market.

The less you respond to negative people, the more peaceful your life will become.

Day 322: How Does the Rent-to-Own Process Work?

Ever hear about the rent-to-own investment strategy and wonder, "How does it work?" An investor decides to market a property as a lease-option or rent-to-own property. The investor finds a qualified tenant/buyer and draws up the terms of an agreement, including monthly rent and final purchase price. Agreements usually last from two to three years. The tenant/buyer provides a down payment, which is usually a lot smaller than what would be required to purchase a home outright. This secures the tenant/buyer's stake in the property and is applied toward the final purchase price. The tenant/buyer pays a standard market monthly rent plus a premium, which is also credited toward the purchase price. At the end of the term, the tenant/buyer has the right to decide if he or she still wants to purchase the property. Either way, the owner benefits from a steady income during the agreement.

We cannot become what we need to be by remaining what we are. Let go of the old you if you want to be the new you.

Day 323: Setup for Recovery

Yes, we are in the password maze each day. Sharing passwords is a bad practice, but especially when so many people reuse passwords between apps and bank accounts. With each application we add to our arsenal, we are required to add one more password to our brain memory bank. With required symbols and alphanumeric combinations being reset after ninety days, the haze is unbearable.

Enter the new password app to save you. With LastPass, your entire collection of passwords is close at hand. You can store, launch, view, or edit entries created with either a tap or a swipe. It's a brilliant tool, with settings for password length and password combos that include uppercase characters, lowercase characters, special characters, or numbers. Try to avoid the use of ambiguous characters (like O and 0), and specify how many numbers to include in the password. Get some help, and keep your head on straight.

Life is like riding a bicycle: to keep your balance, you must keep moving.

Day 324: The Carpenter

If knowledge is king, then your options are endless to become part of the royal family. Add wiki-How, Snapguide, and iHandy Carpenter to your growing knowledge base. Try all the apps and websites packed with how-to advice. In one session you can find some shortcuts for your next project. RoomScan Pro takes advantage of your smartphone's motion sensors to quickly scan and record your room and floor plan layouts. Simply tap your smartphone on the wall and wait for the beep, repeating on each wall and door frame that you want to record. Save floor plans into images, PDF, and DXF files. There may be fees if you need more advanced export options. Wiki-How provides you with thousands of how-to guides, ranging from tech and life hacks to quick repairs, and has complete illustrations and videos. Have some fun.

Train your mind to see good in everything.

Day 325: Ever Hear the Old Saying about a "Blessing and a Curse"?

Unlimited information waits at your fingertips. All you have to do is reach into your pocket. Processes that used to take hours sitting behind a desk can now be completed in seconds while on the go. Mobile device technology allows you to stay connected almost anywhere in the world. This also means that when some renters contact you about a request, they expect an answer "yesterday," as the saying goes. Caribbean vacations or family events such as weddings or even funerals might not be enough to dissuade certain tenants from calling if they decide an issue is pressing enough. Fair or not, the country is well into the "microwave generation." People have grown accustomed to immediate results and immediate responses. Tenants are no different. Try to respond to tenant requests at the earliest possible opportunity to meet reasonable expectations.

It's your life. Don't let anyone make you feel guilty for living it your way.

Day 326: Wowing Quality Tenants

Marketing professionals across the country note the shift in recent years in customer expectations. Consumers used to focus mainly on the quality of products and services. Now customers pay for "experiences." Remember that tenants are also consumers, and the physical living space should only be a part of the package you offer. Today's tenants are looking for the "wow factor." Deliver something unique and valuable to keep your clients renewing each year. Work with a friend to determine all that is right and good about your building and your location. Reduce your turnover by delivering to that experience. For example, if your rental is close to a public-transit station, offer renewal-based gifts such as new earbuds or an iTunes gift card for those long commutes. It's not hard to find low-cost ways to exceed expectations.

Never let waiting become a habit. Live your dreams and take risks. Life is happening now.

Day 327: A Form for All Seasons

Why wait to fax or e-mail out a PDF application? Set up a prescreening application form with Google Forms and enjoy the added benefit of sharing the results with your team. Results are stored in a spreadsheet-style set of results stored in Google Drive where your team can perform verification of the responses and move quickly to expedite the screening process. E-mail alerts are sent as each new application is received. Consider adding forms for employer and previous landlord verification. Expediting your process is not the only benefit. You now add backup files with results and date/time stamps on each application. Search through the templates to find forms for invitations, maintenance requests, and timecards.

Don't be ashamed of your story. It will inspire others.

Day 328: A Tablet a Day

Your tablet, your best project companion, is small and portable and has long battery life. Tablets add true value to scouting properties and evaluating deals, from pictures to movies to special-analysis calculators. Set up your e-signature and pack it up to complete your day on the move. From opening applications to lease signing, it makes reading everything quick and simple. It's superfast and easy for everyone to read if you're at a house site reviewing the scope of your project with the contractors. Track progress, take pictures, and send updates out with a simple click.

Memories take us back; dreams take us forward.

Day 329: Who Needs "Snail Mail," You Say?

Some people jokingly speculate that technology will make postal services go the way of the dinosaur. Despite the speed and convenience of marketing through e-mail, text messages, Facebook pages, tweets, and the like, there are some things technology alone just can't do. For example, direct-mail marketing is one of the best ways to target customers by geographical area. You can use a small local printer, try the inexpensive postcard services available through websites, or search for an affordable, automated-mail lead-generation service. These services offer the streamlined efficiency of scheduling up to a year's worth of monthly mailings or the more accessible feel of a postcard arriving in a mailbox. Digital technology is an awesome time-saver, but it will never completely replace old-fashioned paper and ink. Examine how print-mail marketing can benefit your business before you write it off (pardon the pun).

Life is not always perfect. Like a road, it has many bends and ups and downs, but that's its beauty.

Day 330: You Can Do What the Big Guys Do

Sometimes small-scale investors get bogged down by thinking they have to do it all themselves. Or they believe only the big guys can afford to hire out services to expand a business and make it run more smoothly. Just because you know how to do a task doesn't always mean you should, and there are some services you can hardly afford *not* to delegate. Consider the example of running a consistent direct-mail campaign to target your desired area. Large-scale investors subscribe to sophisticated services to generate productive leads. Small investors recognize the value of these types of campaigns. The most important part is to track what's working. For example, simply send out two sets of postcards with two messages, each having a different link to your website. This will allow you to verify the statistics to indicate which campaign has been most successful.

Life doesn't come with any guarantees. You have to risk it to get the biscuit.

Day 331: Determining Lease Terms for Commercial Tenants

Owners of commercial properties face different and sometimes more complex decisions when filling vacancies than residential property owners. Not only do commercial owners have to take into account the tenant's income and previous rental history, they also have to pin down many variables relating to how the lease will be structured.
How long will the lease term be? Will it be based on gross income or net income? How often will the lease be adjusted based on a rent review? The owner should have a strong idea of what terms will be most favorable to him or her long before meeting with a potential client. Allow room for flexibility if minor adjustments need to be made for the convenience of a good prospect, but make sure you know and honor your boundaries of profitability.

*Choose love and joy as much as you can in each moment,
and watch your life transform.*

Day 332: Recognizing the Right Client for Your Commercial Vacancy

Always recognize the importance of finding the right applicant for the space when selecting a tenant for a commercial property vacancy. The first tenant who can meet your income requirements might not always be the best fit for the long term. Does the client's business complement or clash with those of your existing tenants? Is the surrounding area likely to support the business and allow the client to pay the rent on time? Even if the business operated successfully at another location, it's important to know if your property can allow the client to generate the same level of income. One would expect the prospective tenant to do all the business research before choosing your location, but you, as the landlord, should do your own research. You have almost as much to lose as the commercial tenant whose business can't survive at your property. Protect yourself by doing your homework.

Life is 10 percent what happens to us and 90 percent how we react to it.

Day 333: Security Deposits and the Law

Most states require you, as a landlord, to refund your tenant's security deposit in full or with all the necessary deductions, with an itemized list giving a breakdown of the deductions. Failing to do so may result in a fine, which can be as high as three times the amount of deposit. The time limit within which you need to provide the refund varies from state but state, but it is a mandatory requirement.

You are allowed to deduct the following items from the security deposit:

- unpaid rent
- repairs for damage other than normal wear and tear
- in some states, fees for cleaning a rental unit after move-out, but only to the level of cleanliness at the time of move-in
- in some states, a fee to replace or restore personal property, such as keys to the unit

You may not withhold money from the security deposit for the following items:

- the cost of repairing defects that existed prior to the tenants moving in
- conditions in the rental unit caused by normal wear and tear
- extra cleaning, if the unit is as clean as it was when it was rented

It's better if you become familiar with the laws in your state and understand them well. It's not worth having to pay a fine because you missed some fine print or did not understand some clause. Check your local codes and laws.

Not everything will go as you expect in your life. This is why you need to drop expectations and go with the flow of life.

Day 334: The Security-Deposit Deduction

As a landlord, deducting from your tenant's security deposit for the wrong reasons—for damage the tenant did not cause—or being late on returning it could earn you a penalty up to three times the security-deposit value. Therefore, you need to understand the laws of the state you live in and understand legalese, such as "normal wear" versus "damage" because this can mean the difference between a penalty for you or refunds paid by the tenant to you.

For example, you can charge for damage caused to the rental unit but not for normal wear and tear. The laws do not define "normal wear and tear," but it is the natural deterioration of the unit that occurs during normal conditions. Think of it as harm that occurs during living in, cleaning, and maintaining the rental unit, such as frayed carpets, worn tile, faded paint, and so forth. Damage, on the other hand, is a result of an accident or an unreasonable use of your rental unit, such as walls with holes, broken windows, and accumulation of dirt.

An occupation-related comparison is useful here. Consider the joint pains that a construction worker experiences as a result of daily work versus a fracture the worker sustains from a beam falling on his or her arm. The former is "normal wear and tear" and does not require damage compensation, whereas the latter does.

There's no room to be careless—the devil lies in the details. Nothing can beat meticulous records.

Don't cry over the past; it's gone. Don't stress about the future; it hasn't arrived. Live in the present and make it beautiful.

Day 335: Visual Documentation to Beat Extra Costs Later

When you rent your house out, take photos of the state of the house with your cell phone or digital camera. Including a copy of the day's newspaper visible in each frame will prove the date the photo was taken. Small-claims-court judges may not accept camera-date stamps as documentation because they can be altered. This will provide proof of the baseline state of the house. Note all preexisting damage. Make a checklist, and give it to your tenant with lines for date and signature. Your state may require you to do this. Protect yourself and the tenant from the quirks of unpredictable human nature. You won't be able to claim wrongful damage, and the tenant won't be able to claim negligence or lack of fulfillment on your side. It's better to leave no room for unnecessary accusations and counteraccusations.

Set out in writing and sign the changes that you plan to make in the house before you sign the lease and rent it out. This will prevent you from getting into trouble later if the tenant claims that certain promised changes/repairs were not done. Document repairs that are made by the tenant during the stay, as well as your repairs during that time. Make sure that you make a proper survey of the house when the tenant vacates, compare it to the earlier checklist, and state that you have documented the property's condition. Ensure that you know what you are liable for and what your tenant is liable for repairing.

If you follow these steps, you can help to avoid nasty legal battles resulting from some oversight on either your part or the tenant's. This will prove cheaper in the long term and avoid any bad blood between you and the tenant.

I like criticism. It makes you strong.

—LeBron James

Day 336 Should You Use Skip Tracing?

Skip-tracing services track down people who have "skipped town." They use technology to find those who seem to have disappeared. Such services have long been used in debt collections, finding heirs, and similar applications.

Should you use these services? Do the math. That is what your answer as a real estate investor should be when considering using any service that is available. So, does it add up? Well, if it's regarding the Buckingham Palace or the White House, it may be a complete no-brainer. But if it's for chasing down runaway renters, step carefully. What is the guarantee of finding the right person? When it comes to tenants who owe back rent, the skip-tracing fee would just be the beginning of a long line of expenses. Again, do the math. If Google and social networks can help solve your problem, then get started. That's the golden rule: do the math.

> I'm reflective only in the sense that I learn to move forward. I reflect with a purpose.
>
> —Kobe Bryant

Day 337: Keep Evolving

As human beings, we are never static. We are always changing. This is a fact of life. And as a result of that, things we interact with also keep changing. The same can be said about the real estate market because it deals with places where humans stay. There are always some new trends, new styles, and new demands coming in. Thus, as a seller, you have to keep sharpening the axe. Keep ensuring that your skills and knowledge set are up to date. As with new laws, new technology, new business changes, new markets, and new industries will keep coming up. All these changes matter—they tell you where there are prospective houses and prospective sellers, where you might make a killing, and where you should back out. It's believed that you need to do something for ten thousand hours before you become good at it. That should be your understanding and target. If you put in the effort, you will be unbeatable in your field—be it real estate investing or cleaning toilets.

> Plant your own gardens and decorate your own soul,
> instead of waiting for someone to bring you flowers.

Day 338: Should Virtual Reality Be a Part of Your Real Estate Strategy?

Virtual reality (VR) is convenient. Buyers will be happy and relaxed once they realize exactly what they are buying and know what the problems will be. Imagine if you went out on a date and had a software program that could look into the future and tell you how your relationship would play out. Get the idea? That's what we are discussing here. As George Costanza would say, "It is the future." Don't think that VR is some pie in the sky when you die. It's the future that has arrived. There was a time when computers were only available to governments and big businesses. Thus, it's easy to see that VR might follow the same path and become a part of everyday life. New technology will incorporate more features into VR to make it the complete experience. Getting started with VR now will set you apart from the crowd—you may be the only person in the area offering this product. Let your clients see you as tech savvy and in tune with the times. Basically, being up to date says that you are a person worth doing business with.

> Never get so busy making a living that you forget to make a life.

Day 339: Be an Early Adopter Pioneer

What if you could let prospects experience the house and "live" in it without actually living in it? What if they could experience the house exactly as it was—see the view from the bay window, determine how the tables and curtains should be placed, and estimate the amount of sunlight in each area of the house? Well, guess what? That is soon going to happen. In fact, it is already happening.

Samsung Gear and Google's Oculus Rift are being used by premium house sellers to give house previews to buyers—who happen to be spending millions on these homes and would like to know that their money is being well spent. As Matthew J. Leone, the senior vice president of digital marketing for Terra Holdings, says, "We sell based on emotion and attaching that emotion to a vision. Imagine a buyer walking out onto the terrace and thinking, 'If I bought this home and was having breakfast here, this is exactly what I'd see.' That's incredible. For a salesperson, it's a dream come true."

Firms are adopting this new and unique method of selling houses. This technology will transform the real estate industry once again. Saying that house shopping will become more efficient would be the understatement of the century. The next project in the pipeline is to incorporate touch and smell in the house to make the experience more authentic. Soon you will be able to not just see the new house but also touch and feel the furniture and smell the roses.

Success is not the key to happiness. Happiness is the key to success. If you love what you are doing, you will be successful.

Day 340: Keeping It All Together

"Now, what did I do with that lease agreement and security-deposit receipt?" the landlord mumbles while the new tenant waits expectantly. Tenants notice things like this, and you do *not* want to give the wrong impression. A disorganized landlord does not inspire confidence as someone who can effectively manage the mechanical, legal, financial, and human aspects of running a successful rental business. A well-organized landlord should be able to put his or her hands on any important document stored on-site within five minutes. Not only is the need to search for the documents to run your business a waste of time, it shows that your operations could use a tune-up. Keep your items on hand when you need them, and file them properly when you don't. No tenant ever wants to see you patting down your shabby old raincoat like an absent-minded Columbo.

All progress takes place outside the comfort zone.

Day 341: Is It Possible You've Been "Yelped," and You Didn't Even Know It?

Remember the adage, "Bad news travels fast"? If you meet a renter for a showing and you're polite, professional, and neatly dressed as you present a well-kept rental unit, that renter might go tell three people about the positive experience. If you show up late, are sloppily dressed, and have a rude manner while showing a filthy unit, you might become the subject of a story told for years to come. And consider that wonderful tool called the Internet, which makes our lives so much easier. If a renter posts a comment about you, it could reach thousands over time—and you might never even know it. Word of mouth is a two-way street. Bad comments about you and your rental can spread just the same way that good comments can spread—usually at a much faster rate. Protect your reputation by keeping it professional.

> The best way to predict your future is to create it.
>
> —ABRAHAM LINCOLN

Day 342: Trust Is Hard to Gain and Easy to Lose

If you give tenants a reason to question your integrity, it could be very difficult to win that trust back. Don't take a chance. Don't hide problems such as security issues or pest sightings. Be honest and transparent as you work to solve situations. Not only is it the right of the residents to know about conditions in the building that might affect them, it also shows that you respect them as human beings. You're all adults, and residents are just as smart as you are. It's true that renters of your properties might sometimes insult your intelligence with some scheme or another. But think of how annoying it is to you when a resident thinks he or she is pulling the wool over your eyes. It works the same in reverse. Ultimately, people can tell when your methods and your approach are not aboveboard.

If it excites you and scares you at the same time, it might be a good thing to try.

Day 343: No Pushovers or Stuffed Shirts Allowed

Everyone knows a good property owner should avoid being a "doormat landlord." That's the landlord who consistently allows late payments, turns a blind eye to unauthorized occupants, and doesn't charge for damages caused by the tenant. Obviously, you never want to become "that guy" or "that girl." It can be equally problematic, though, if you become the landlord who never bends. Have you ever been late on a payment for anything? Have you ever been frustrated by the delay of a payment you were expecting? Have you ever had an unforeseen expense that required you to make some difficult choices for your personal finances? Things like this happen to the best of us. If a resident has a good payment history, don't start eviction proceedings after the first late payment. Cut just a little slack, and give the tenant a chance to resolve the issue.

The difference between who you are and who you want to be is what you do.

Day 344: "My Landlord Said He'll Get around to It...Someday"

The running toilet becomes the nightly lullaby in a family's otherwise quiet unit. The doorknob to the linen closet comes off in the tenant's hand every time he or she is ready for a fresh towel. The smoke detector in the hallway chirps constantly like some deranged exotic bird. Even minor maintenance issues can do a lot to damage landlord-tenant relationships when left for too long. This is a major gripe for tenants. Unaddressed service requests not only inconvenience tenants, they also give tenants the impression that they are not valued as "customers." Fulfill service requests quickly. Correct the problem yourself or call in the services of a professional, but make sure the work is done well. This will go a long way toward retaining the good tenants you already have as well as attracting new ones.

Change happens when the pain of staying the same is greater than the pain of change.

Day 345: Spice Up Your Hardware

One thing is certain about our generation. We are living in an age of ultimate convenience. Almost anything we want is available at the swipe of a finger or flick of the wrist. Hence, as a real estate investor whose business needs functionality and convenience, it's not a bad idea to see what is available that you can buy now or sometime in the future based on your budget. Here are some hardware options:

- *USB-C plugs.* USB-C plugs are slowly replacing the current standard USB-A plug in most new computers. They can connect to all devices and handle charging, data transfer, and external displays better, and they are more power efficient. USB-C may become the future standard, so remember that when upgrading your business devices.
- *Three hundred and sixty-degree cameras.* Several companies are releasing models of 360-degree cameras that cost well below $1,000, such as Kodak's Pixpro SP360 4K Action Cam for $500. These are portable and can provide an expanded view of your listings.
- *Big add-ons to small homewares.* Nowadays, there's no need to buy expensive devices, because smartphones are making it easier to sync most devices together—for example, light bulbs that stream music (Sengled Pulse light bulb) and carbon-monoxide detectors that send alerts to your phone.

Advances such as these are making new technology accessible at very affordable prices. So, it's time to pimp up your business, impress your customers, and enjoy convenience at the same time.

> Don't set your goals by what other people deem important.

Day 346: Amazing New Software

There is nothing soft about software. It packs a powerful punch when it comes to efficiency and productivity. There are many software products that can help boost your business. Connectivity is the buzzword of the twenty-first century—people want to connect anything to anything and everything.

The Internet of Things is a term that describes how companies are making products with components that connect them to the Internet. Examples include Samsung's SmartThings platform, which connects more than two hundred household devices, and others such as Lowe's Iris, LG's Smart thinQ, Amazon's Echo, and Panasonic's Ora.

Vast amounts of automation are happening in our lives; we might soon have an app to complete our daily shower! Till then, we have to make do with automations that ease the pains of doing business. YouMail, for example, answers your calls. A little bit of automation may ease your work and improve your efficiency. Apple's Siri has transformed the ugly duckling of voice control into the emperor swan of this decade. Soon, all products—from door locks to appliances—will operate through voice control. The errors in voice control dropped from 23 percent in 2013 to 5 percent in 2015. It won't be long until the keyboard has gone the way of the cassette.

Lifestyle design takes conscious choice.

Day 347: Zillow's Owner Dashboard

Owner Dashboard is the latest tool brought out by Zillow for real estate agents, whether they advertise on Zillow or not. It's useful in enhancing a listing's exposure on the site. It offers home sellers a clear window into how their listing is engaging people online. It allows consumers to converse with the agent regarding the marketability of the house. Anyone can view unclaimed listings on the dashboard, but you have to enter the correct homeowner's name for listed postings. It encourages the addition of more home facts and photos, based on which the value of the home is calculated. This new app seems poised to set the market on fire.

Along with Owner's Dashboard, Zillow has rolled out two tools that are nestled in the dashboard: Price Your Home, a home-valuation tool that lets users compare homes and prices, and Best Time to List, which estimates how much the timing of a listing affects the price. Users are also able to explore Zillow's new Sale Proceeds Calculator, which calculates the net profit of a home's sale. The Zillow Premier Agent app allows agents to buy more ads from the listing portal by making it easier to manage leads. By allowing uploading of walk-through videos, the portal has incentivized the downloading of the app. Appearances in listing-search results are boosted by videos, which can now only be shot with the downloaded Zillow app. Take a look at Zillow for details.

Success seems to be connected with action. Successful people keep moving. They make mistakes. But they don't quit.

Day 348: The Flyp App

Fed up with having to juggle multiple phones and multiple phone numbers? Don't know which number is meant for what purpose? Getting disturbed during family time by business calls? You may even be carrying multiple phones in your pocket, exposing yourself to radiation—the existence of which phone companies deny but may result in your kids having ten fingers on each hand.

This is where Flyp can help. What is it, exactly? It lets you have five numbers on a single smartphone. Yes, you heard it right: five! And no, it's not even Christmas. It can function on both of the main platforms, iOS and Android. A Flyp account allows users to set up five additional phone numbers on an iPhone or Android. Your current number makes six. New users request the desired area code and are offered a list of available numbers from which to choose. The app has numbers in close to 90 percent of all US area codes. Each number is assigned almost like a separate identity on the phone, with a separate color, a custom name, and individual settings. The app can be used for texting as well. Perhaps the app's smartest feature is Conversations. This streamlined interface consolidates all phone and text communications with contacts by their Flyp numbers in a clear visual timeline. Flyp stands out among business apps for its practicality, elegance, and sales applicability.

The way to get started is to quit talking and begin doing.

Day 349: How One Rental Market Grows Every Day

Would you believe estimates say that about ten thousand baby boomers turn sixty-five in the United States *every day*? And that this rate is expected to continue for at least another dozen years? That's what the Pew Research Center, the premier nonpartisan entity tracking demographic trends in American society, found in a recent survey. How's that for a market trend? Add to that the fact that boomers (those born in the post–World War II years between 1946 and 1964) make up roughly one quarter of the population, and your investor's intuition will tell you that the power of these numbers can't be underestimated.

Some investors take advantage by buying shares in real estate investment trusts for large and highly profitable nursing homes and assisted-living facilities. Other investors might create a smaller-scale business model based on owning and operating smaller assisted-living facilities. There are many options for tapping into this trend.

Understanding what you value most will help simplify even the most complex decisions.

Day 350: Affordable Senior Housing: a Growing Niche

America's population is aging, and every segment of society will be affected in some way. Aside from health care, one area that will see the biggest changes is housing for older Americans. Existing housing is woefully inadequate to meet unique needs of older Americans, according to a Harvard University report, "Housing America's Older Adults: Meeting the Needs of an Aging Population." A huge factor for seniors is affordability. The price of market-rate housing options is outpacing many seniors' ability to afford independent living. The study shows that one-third of adults over fifty devoted at least 30 percent of their income to housing costs, and almost ten million seniors paid over half of their income to rents or mortgages. This can lead to tough choices about foregoing basic needs. Real estate investors can contribute to society by providing affordable senior housing to meet the sharply growing demand.

When was the last time you did something for the first time?

Day 351: Providing Accessibility in Senior Housing Improves Quality of Life

More people in their advancing years are unable to drive or choose not to drive. Some cities and towns operate good public-transportation systems. Overall, though, most residential areas cater to the convenience of drivers by chance or by design. Also, harsh weather conditions and fear of crime can present a barrier to using public transportation even in areas where good systems exist. One result is isolation from family and friends. In addition to limited options of traveling by way of vehicles, physical mobility challenges also cause older Americans to feel confined to their living spaces. Many seniors at the same time face health challenges that require more frequent trips to the doctor. The combination of these factors leads to a much greater need for senior housing that integrates on-site access to health-care services and proximity to family and friends.

People who succeed have momentum. The more they want to succeed, the more they find a way to succeed.

Day 352: Benefits of the Assisted-Living-Facility Business Model

Assisted-living facilities (ALFs), *assisted-living residences*, and *board and care* are all terms that describe a housing alternative for seniors who do not require the high-level medical care of full-scale nursing homes. Residents are "assisted" with daily activities, such as eating, bathing, dressing, and using the toilet. Buy-and-hold investors who specialize in the traditional approach of renting homes to single families might consider some of the benefits of switching or expanding to ALFs. Multiple unrelated residents in the same living space spread out their risk of delinquent rents and vacancies. Selecting a property based on the best all-important cash-flow numbers in this business model decreases the need to buy the lowest-priced property. Also, the return on this type of investment can produce a good yield for an investor without the need to own many properties. This is a great option for the investor who prefers a smaller portfolio.

If you are not willing to risk the unusual, you will have to settle for the ordinary.

—Jim Rohn

Day 353: What Types of Properties Are the Best Options for Assisted-Living Facilities?

If your goal is to buy properties to operate as ALFs, some choices are better than others. A single-level residence (for instance, a ranch-style home) reduces the inconvenience and risk of climbing stairs. A home with a larger square footage provides more elbow room for multiple residents. Wide, open spaces and hallways make it easier to navigate wheelchairs and walking assistive devices. Although the number of bedrooms has always been one of the most attractive features for homebuyers, the number of bathrooms is what catches the eye of the ALF investor. It's much cheaper and easier to convert space (including attached garages) into additional bedrooms than it is to add plumbing for additional bathrooms. Upper-middle-class areas tend to attract more ALF renters. Finally, before buying, find out if your state limits the number of units one ALF can hold.

> Success is walking from failure to failure with no loss of enthusiasm.

Day 354: What Makes the Most Marketable Assisted-Living Facility?

With units having an average annual cost of $45,000, residents of ALFs have every right to expect to get their money's worth. What are some features of the best ALFs?
Like anyone, seniors value their independence and self-sufficiency. Requiring assistance for small daily tasks can be humbling. Having patient and compassionate staff in place eases discomfort. Some residents choose assisted living as an alternative to what they perceive as the impersonal nature of large nursing homes. ALFs should reflect a more intimate, casual atmosphere than that of a big institution. The convenience of a private bedroom along with home-cooked meals in a communal dining arrangement combines the best of both worlds. The investor who operates ALFs has to factor in a deeper level of customer service as a result of being more intimately connected with the daily lives of renters.

A creative person is motivated by the desire to achieve, not by the desire to beat others.

Day 355: Don't Be a Victim of TLDR

Have you ever received an e-mail that you knew had some significance, but it sat unread in your inbox for days or even weeks? Don't worry. You're far from being alone. In fact, this phenomenon has become so popular that pop culture has slapped a name on it. You can file these unwieldy messages under the header TLDR, or "too long, didn't read." Communicating with tenants, property managers, contractors, mortgage brokers, home inspectors, accountants, attorneys, and others is a crucial part of running an effective rental business. Don't assume that people will take the time to read a long correspondence just because they have received your message. Good communication doesn't just involve sending a message. Effective communication requires you to increase the chances that the message will be read, understood, and answered—in a timely manner.

There will always be a reason why you meet people. Either you need to change your life, or you are the one who will change theirs.

Day 356: How to Write an Effective E-Mail

Contrary to popular belief, writing short, effective messages actually takes more time than writing long messages. The higher response rate, however, makes that extra effort much more than worth it. Making sure you clearly convey the action you want the receiver to take makes it much more likely that the receiver will comply. Use your subject line as an effective tool to detail yet summarize your message. Avoid including additional details. Be brief, generic, and professional. Overly friendly e-mails and texts are not appropriate for business. Handle your e-mail communications as if you are writing to a banker or a lawyer. Aim to limit messages to five sentences or less. Include the most important information first. Keep in mind that a shorter, well-thought-out message implies a respect for the value of your recipient's time. Bulleted or numbered lists are best when communicating specific action items that need to be addressed. Applying these tips will reduce the need to go back and forth with your recipient.

Life is only as good as your mind-set.

Day 357: Simplify Your Life with Property-Management Software

Most property-management software programs have been specifically developed to automate tasks that bog down personnel at large management companies handling the holdings of huge investment companies. If you're a "solopreneur," then you *are* your company's personnel! You have even more of a need to streamline your processes than an employee in a multiple-person shop. And add to that the fact that landlords are always on the go—when you're conducting showings, buying supplies, or resolving tenant disputes, you need technology that allows you to take your information with you. The right property-management software lets you carry tons of information around in your pocket. At the touch of your smartphone screen, software products allow you to review applications, screen tenants, and list available properties. Whether you go it alone or hire a manager, using management software can make some of the most tedious processes a breeze.

Difficult roads often lead to a beautiful destination.

Day 358: Software to Make You the Apple of Your Accountant's Eye

The ability to communicate with tenants and the ease of scheduling appointments are great features of most property-management software systems. However, using the great accounting functions of many systems is what will make your tax professional adore you forever. Eliminate double-entry errors through live error-checking features. Reducing errors not only leads to greater accuracy, it also saves a ton of time that can be spent on other projects. The ability to produce regular reports allows you to keep up with your figures all year and reduces the need to reconcile numbers just before you file. Forget trying to create your own spreadsheets. Put the old-fashioned pen and paper in a drawer. Making your accountant's job easier at tax time is the gift that keeps on giving—back to *you!*

You will never influence the world by trying to be like it.

Day 359: More Ways Tenants Benefit from Property-Management Software

Property-management software benefits tenants in more ways than just allowing for online rent payments. Tenant portals also give residents the 24-7 convenience of submitting service requests or reviewing the terms of their leases. Residents can find out if a payment has been credited or if their rent balance is current. Miscommunications and loss of vital details can occur when requests are placed by residents to an operator who then passes the info on to the owner. Online service requests allow residents to give details in their own words. This provides efficient channels of communication between residents and the management company. Moreover, the owner has a bird's-eye view of all communication exchanges for peace of mind that issues are being handled in a timely manner.

If you never try, you will never know.

Day 360: Bringing Tenants Up to Date about Online Payments

If the days of mailing in rent payments are going the way of the Model T Ford, face-to-face rent collecting might have already gone the way of the dinosaur. If any tenants of your properties are hesitant about online payments or if they don't have easy access to a computer, it's worth it for you to take the time to explain the benefits. Not only are online payments faster than other methods, they can also be more secure. Tenants can avoid the hassle and expense of purchasing money orders, stamps, and envelopes. Tenants who don't have a computer in the home can make payments through a smartphone, at work, or by accessing a computer on their next local public library visit. Usher your tenants into a brand-new day. Once they get the hang of it, they'll be glad you did.

The only person you should try to be better than is the person you were yesterday.

Day 361: Using Social Media as a Tool for Your Business

Social media platforms, which started as a way for loved ones who were separated by distance or were too tied to busy schedules to keep in touch, have been commandeered by the business world. Building your presence on social media allows for you to have "constant contact" with people in your investor network. Landlords can keep current residents informed and attract prospective renters. Wholesalers and rehabbers can attract new buyers and sellers and maintain connections to previous buyers and sellers to generate referrals. And there's no need to direct your efforts toward one platform. What if your resident Amy gets all her updates on LinkedIn, your tenant Gary likes Twitter, prospective renter Louis could not live without Facebook, and future buyer Leslie still hangs on to her MySpace account? Software such as Hootsuite lets you release a message through multiple social channels all at once.

In the end, we only regret the chances we didn't take.

Day 362: Property-Management Software to Weed Out Bad Tenants

Whether you view your property with the sentimental fondness of an investor's first purchase or with the detached feeling of an income-generating tool to reach your financial goals, protecting your property is important to you. Installing security systems and smoke alarms is one route, but an equally important way to do that is by carefully selecting the people you allow to occupy your space. Instant reports on tenant screenings and background checks reduce wasted time for owners, leasing agents, and property managers, as well as prospective tenants. On-demand access to information on eviction history, credit, and criminal records helps you quickly determine who is financially responsible and more likely to cooperate with the lease terms. The faster you get the negative responses to the tenants who don't qualify, the faster you can move on to the positive ones.

Don't call it a dream; call it a plan.

Day 363: Don't Get Lost in the Woods

Motivational speaker Brendon Burchard often quotes the old Montana saying, "The time you want the map is before you enter the woods," meaning you should plan out your journey before you even get started. Having a plan gives you a reference point to return to even if you get sidetracked or stray from your path. Not having a plan could leave you lost among the trees. You could spend months or even years working hard, with your head down, putting in a lot of effort. Then you might look up one day and see you haven't really gotten any closer to your goal. This is the situation where some investors get frustrated and give up. It's not that they're unwilling to put in the hard work. It's just that lack of a plan won't focus that hard work into a successful outcome. Make your hard work pay off.

If your dreams don't scare you, they aren't big enough.

Day 364: The Stages of Growth for Your Business

You've taken on that crucial task of creating a real plan for your business. Congratulations on following through with that all-important step that many investors skip. You're setting yourself up for much success in your investing career. When that success comes, make sure you've prepared yourself for it. Believe it or not, some investors fear success even as they work hard to achieve it. As long as you create an effective plan and stay focused on it, you'll be just fine. Always keep in mind the steps you can take to grow your business to the next level. Add these ideas to your plan where feasible. Your business plan should be organic. It should live and grow along with your business. Look forward to your growth with excitement and enthusiasm. Your hard work *will* pay off, and building on your success is the key to maintaining momentum.

Sometimes you win; sometimes you learn.

Day 365: Success Has Arrived! What's the Next Step for Your Business?

Part of the fun of investing is watching the plans you made bear fruit and then coming up with bigger and better plans going forward. You bought your first rental property. Great! Now how many more will you buy in the next six months? You taught yourself to be an expert and cornered the market in your neighborhood. Awesome! Now how soon can you expand your portfolio to include properties in the surrounding area? You bought three single-family homes this year. Phenomenal! Next year, what can you do to buy three single-family homes each month? Competence builds confidence. Once you learn the mechanics of a particular process, you develop an appreciation for your own abilities. As you gain experience, watch yourself get much more comfortable with setting your sights higher.

Be a Part of Secure Pay One's Landlord Legacy

Send us a story, a challenge you faced, or a new technology you love, and we will send you a free "New Tenant Welcome Booklet" template for your business.

E-mail us: spoinfo1@gmail.com

Sign up for our newsletter at www.securepayone.com/contact_us

If you would like to focus on a new quote to start each day, sign up spoinfo1@gmail.com

Find us:
LinkedIn: Linda Liberatore
Facebook: www.facebook.com/securepayone
Twitter: www.twitter.com/securepayone

Disclaimer

The information contained in this book is strictly for educational purposes. It is not intended to be professional legal advice. Never rely on the information presented in this book in place of seeking professional legal advice. Every effort has been made to accurately represent current information in the materials presented. Laws vary by state, city, and municipality, and they should be reviewed with your legal counsel.

Made in the USA
San Bernardino, CA
03 August 2016